The Origins of New Testament Christology

# The Origins of
# New Testament Christology

I. Howard Marshall

INTERVARSITY PRESS
DOWNERS GROVE, ILLINOIS 60515

Published in the United States of America by InterVarsity Press, Downers Grove, Illinois, with permission from Universities and Colleges Christian Fellowship, Leicester, England

Originally published in the Issues of Contemporary Interpretation series in 1976

This updated edition first published in 1990

InterVarsity Press is the book-publishing division of InterVarsity Christian Fellowship, a student movement active on campus at hundreds of universities, colleges and schools of nursing in the United States of America, and a member movement of the International Fellowship of Evangelical Students. For information about local and regional activities, write Public Relations Dept., InterVarsity Christian Fellowship, 6400 Schroeder Rd., P.O. Box 7895, Madison, WI 53707-7895.

ISBN 0-8308-1750-6

Printed in Great Britain by Collins, Glasgow

---

**Library of Congress Cataloging in Publication Data**
Marshall, I. Howard.
 The origins of New Testament christology / I. Howard Marshall. – Rev. ed.
 p. cm.
 Includes bibliographical references and index.
 ISBN 0-8308-1305-5
 1. Jesus Christ – History of doctrines – Early church, ca. 30–600.
 2. Jesus Christ – History of doctrines – 20th century.   I. Title.
BT198.M39  1990
232′.09′015 – dc20                                                            90-40484
                                                                                        CIP

---

16   15   14   13   12   11   10   9   8   7   6   5   4   3   2   1

99   98   97   96   95   94   93   92   91   90

# CONTENTS

# PREFACE TO THE FIRST EDITION

This book is concerned with the teaching of the New Testament about the person of Jesus, a subject vast in scope, unencompassable in its bibliography and daunting in its problems. The aim is simply to outline the various approaches to the subject, especially during the last twenty years, to look in more detail at some of the main issues, and to offer some critical comments on them; in the process the faint outline of a route that is worth pursuing may begin to emerge, so that this book may not simply be a 'guide to the debate about Christology' but may also offer a viable approach to the subject.

Since the theme is enormous, the discussion is necessarily limited to one aspect of it. Recent study has been much taken up with the titles used to express the significance of the person of Jesus, and in particular with the development in the use of those titles between the lifetime of Jesus and the writing of the books of the New Testament. It is this area which will occupy the student who reads the current textbooks and monographs rather than 'Paul's view of Jesus' or 'John's view of Jesus', crucial though these latter topics are. In the endeavour to do reasonable justice to the interests of contemporary study, so that this book really is a guide to the current debate, it has been necessary to concentrate attention on this early period in Christian thought and to neglect the contributions of the great New Testament theologians.

A word on the method of discussion followed may not

come amiss. The approach adopted here is that of historical and critical study which examines the evidence provided in the New Testament and attempts to evaluate it in its own light. The student of theology has nothing to fear from an open and honest evaluation of the evidence if he believes that all truth is God's truth. Where we differ from the understanding of the evidence adopted by other students, it is our duty to show how and why their understanding is wrong, instead of merely making dogmatic statements. Sometimes, their historical understanding may be at fault – the meaning of a difficult text may elude them; at other times, we may feel that their presuppositions are at fault – as, for example, when the possibility of the supernatural is categorically excluded. In both cases nothing is gained by mere protest; we need to show that our understanding is better founded. And of course we must always be prepared to learn from those from whom we differ; the misunderstandings are not necessarily all on one side! Recognition of this fact will explain why many statements in this book are qualified by a 'probably', even when they concern matters that may seem to some readers to be beyond all doubt. But what may seem to be beyond doubt in terms of religious faith may not be capable of knockdown historical proof, and it is in terms of historical investigation that often we must be content with a 'probably'.

It is usually considered bad form for an author to draw undue attention to his own writings. In the present case the suggestion that I should undertake this book arose on the basis of my own earlier activities in attempting to survey various aspects of Christology. Inevitably, therefore, in writing on the same subject I have had to make use of my earlier efforts in this direction and to repeat some of what has already appeared in *The Evangelical Quarterly, Interpretation, New Testament Studies* and the *Tyndale Bulletin*.

I am grateful to several friends for comments and suggestions, and in particular to Dr R. T. France, Principal of Wycliffe College, Oxford.

# PREFACE TO THE UPDATED EDITION

Since the publication of this book in 1976 the discussion of Christology has continued unabated. When the book appeared in German translation in 1985 (*Die Ursprünge der neutestamentlichen Christologie*, Giessen/Basel: Brunnen Verlag) I took the opportunity to add a brief postscript in which some account is taken of recent studies of the problem. This postscript (with some minor updating) is now added to the updated English edition.

# ABBREVIATIONS

| | |
|---|---|
| *CBQ* | *Catholic Biblical Quarterly* |
| *EQ* | *Evangelical Quarterly* |
| *Exp. T* | *Expository Times* |
| *HTR* | *Harvard Theological Review* |
| *JBL* | *Journal of Biblical Literature* |
| *JTS* | *Journal of Theological Studies* |
| *Nov. T* | *Novum Testamentum* |
| *NTS* | *New Testament Studies* |
| *SJT* | *Scottish Journal of Theology* |
| *SNTSB* | *Society for New Testament Studies Bulletin* |
| *TDNT* | *Theological Dictionary of the New Testament* |
| *TSFB* | *Theological Students' Fellowship Bulletin* |
| *Tyn.B* | *Tyndale Bulletin* |
| *ZNW* | *Zeitschrift für die neutestamentliche Wissenschaft* |
| *ZTK* | *Zeitschrift für Theologie und Kirche* |

Most subjects in biblical and theological study are closely connected with one another, and the person who is rash enough to embark on a study of the person of Jesus Christ will very quickly find himself attempting to cover the whole range of Christian thought stretching over many centuries and encompassing a wide variety of themes. Sheer ignorance, to say nothing of the limited size of the present treatment, compels us to define the limits of our study fairly closely, and even within these chosen limits our discussion must necessarily be fairly sketchy.

On the one hand, the task attempted in this book is a survey of what the New Testament has to say about the person of Christ and how its teaching has been understood by biblical scholars. Much of the modern debate about Christology is concerned with how the data supplied in the New Testament should be utilized in systematic theology or dogmatics: granted that the New Testament says such-and-such about the person of Jesus Christ, how is this evidence to be used in the construction of a modern understanding of him? It goes without saying that the attempt to answer this question is at the very centre of theological discussion, and that the stream of books on the subject is both broad and never-ending. One might well say, 'By their Christologies ye shall know them.' Nevertheless, we must reluctantly lay aside this aspect of the subject.

Our concern is with the task of laying bare what the New Testament says about Jesus, not with what the modern theologian does with the material provided by the New Testament scholar. To be sure, there are numerous examples of contemporary writers who are able to display wide competence in both areas so that their books are contributions both to New Testament study and to systematic theology. One has only to think of W. Pannenberg, *Jesus: God and Man* (1968), or of J. A. T. Robinson, *The Human Face of God* (1973), in the present generation, or of H. R. Mackintosh, *The Doctrine of the Person of Jesus Christ* (1912), in an earlier one, to realize that there are significant studies which contribute richly to both fields of study. Moreover, in view of the contemporary trend in the study of biblical interpretation which insists that attempts to determine what a biblical text meant in the first century and what it has to say to us today cannot be rigidly separated, it is impossible for us to isolate one aspect of the subject from the other; indeed, it will no doubt become apparent in the discussion how much theological presuppositions can be determinative of New Testament exegesis. It must remain the case, however, that our interest in this book is primarily in exegesis, in discovering the nature of the New Testament evidence which forms the raw material for the expositor and the theologian. How the expositor and theologian use it will, it is hoped, be the concern of another author in this series.

On the other hand, our task must be differentiated from that of the historical study of the life of Jesus. Our interest is in what the early church thought about the significance and person of Jesus. For them he was not only a person who lived and worked on the earth, but also a figure whose influence was still present in the world in a way that transcended the manner in which the influence of, say, Socrates might be said to live on after him. A discussion of the earthly ministry of Jesus and its significance would consequently leave out a major part of New Testament thinking on the subject: the effect may be seen by considering how much would be lost if a study of Paul's Christology confined itself purely to what Paul says about the earthly life and teaching of Jesus and stopped short of his resurrection, exaltation and parousia. To be sure, we cannot ignore the question of the earthly life of Jesus and its significance. It has always been a vital question in Christology to discover how far the impact made by the earthly life of Jesus and his own understanding of his person can sustain the weight of the Christological construction put upon them by the early church. We cannot, therefore, in this study ignore the questions of what Jesus said and did, and how far historical study can show the relation between the actual character of his ministry and the theological explanation of it by the early church. We shall, for example, be interested in whether Jesus accepted the title of 'Messiah' as a suitable description of his functions. We want to know how far the use of titles such as 'Son of man' goes back to Jesus himself. But it would go beyond the limits of this study to discuss in any detail the historical problem of how we may scientifically determine what Jesus was 'really' like—and the historiographical and philosophical question of what 'really' really means in this context. These points can receive only a sketchy treatment here, and again a fuller discussion must be sought elsewhere.[1]

The effect of these two qualifications is to define the limits of our subject-matter over against both systematic theology and historical study of the ministry of Jesus. The area that remains is large enough, and all that can be attempted here is to provide the student with a rather small-scale aerial map of the terrain which may help to give a sense of perspective as he trudges over the ground on foot. Our viewpoint is inevitably determined by the current orientation of study: a survey of scholarship in a particular area may not necessarily give a true picture of the area itself, since it must reflect the interests of contemporary students. At the same time the personal bias of the chronicler will make itself felt as he concentrates on those aspects of the subject which he deems to be most significant. The total perspective, therefore, may be faulty, but there are at least some features of the landscape which are bound to show up on almost any kind of aerial photograph, and so it may be hoped that our study may be found to be of some help.

We propose to begin with an over-all view of the subject by looking fairly rapidly at a number of key works which have

appeared over the past century.[2] By this means we shall
introduce ourselves to the main themes and problems of
Christology in the New Testament. Seven writers—a number
not necessarily expressive of perfection or completeness— may
be singled out as characterizing the various phases in modern
study of the subject. Their writings are not necessarily the
most original or creative on the subject, but they will show us
where the principal landmarks in the development of New
Testament interpretation are to be found.

## H. P. Liddon

We begin our survey with *The Divinity of our Lord and
Saviour Jesus Christ* by H. P. Liddon (1829-90). The book,
which was first published in 1867, contains the eight Bampton
Lectures delivered in 1866 on the foundation established by
John Bampton in the University of Oxford. The aim of the
foundation was 'to confirm and establish the Christian faith,
and to confute all heretics and schismatics' and among the
specific items of Christian faith to be confirmed and established was 'the Divinity of our Lord and Saviour Jesus Christ'.
The book runs to some 584 pages, and one notes with relief
that not all of it was read to the patient audience. Liddon's
work produces a thoroughly orthodox view of the person of
Jesus Christ in the New Testament; the reality of his humanity
is accepted with a brief provision of evidence, and all the
emphasis falls upon establishing the fact of his divinity. This
is accomplished in the main by a detailed consideration of
the successful effects of Jesus' ministry and of his self-consciousness, especially as this comes to light in the Gospel of
John. There follows a discussion of the implications of the
prologue to John, and then a statement of the teaching to be
found in the Epistles. Two closing chapters discuss the doctrine to be erected on the basis of the New Testament and the
consequences of the doctrine.

Liddon was no mean scholar and his work is not to be
despised. Indeed, there are still those who would accept it as
a reasonably sufficient statement of the New Testament
evidence at the present time. The typical orthodox exposition
of our subject follows the lines laid down by Liddon, and so

his book is well suited to come first in our survey as the out-
standing example of conservative orthodoxy. It was certainly
not written in ignorance of the challenge which was beginning
to be felt from other quarters by orthodoxy. Liddon was well
aware of the position stated by Lessing: 'If Christ is not truly
God, the Mohammedan religion would be unquestionably an
improvement on the Christian, and Mahomet himself an in-
comparably greater and worthier person than Christ.'[3]

Liddon was also familiar with the full-scale exposition of a
different view of the evidence in the works of D. F. Strauss
and E. Renan, and he makes some attempt to grapple with it,
although it must be admitted that his attempts do not amount
to very much. He is content to rest his case on the infallibility
of Scripture. He does recognize the importance of justifying
his use of the evidence drawn from the Gospel of John and
devotes some pages to a defence of its apostolic authorship,
but he never really delves into the difficulty posed by the
difference between John and the other three Gospels in their
accounts of the teaching of Jesus. For the most part he is content to record the teaching of Jesus and of the New Testament
writers without much sense of history. He is not concerned
with the problem of how the New Testament writers came to
hold their convictions, and he displays none of the interest in
the period between the death of Jesus and the writing of the
earliest books of the New Testament which figures so largely
in modern historical reconstructions of the earliest, pre-literary
period in the early church. Liddon's book is thus unsatisfying
to the modern student because it has not attempted to meet
the sceptical challenge on its own ground by showing that the
orthodox can appeal to history with as much right as the
sceptical. The true way foward was to be shown by a contemporary of Liddon's, Joseph Barbour Lightfoot (1828-89), who
had already published one year earlier in 1865 the first of a
series of volumes (it was a commentary on Galatians) in which
the historical method of study was applied to the vindication
of apostolic Christianity.

## W. Bousset

If Liddon marks the end of the old era, the coming of age of the new is marked by the work of W. Bousset (1865-1920) and especially by the publication of *Kyrios Christos* (1913; a revised edition appeared posthumously in 1921). Liddon remains largely unknown, except in conservative circles. The work of Bousset lives on; it appeared in a fifth edition in 1964 (with a preface by R. Bultmann, who shared in the editing of the 1921 edition), and it attained the honour of an English translation by J. E. Steely as recently as 1970.[4]

Bousset was a rationalist, inheriting the tradition in critical scholarship which attempts to explain the rise of Christianity without any reference to the supernatural. This meant that he saw no special significance from the historical point of view in the canonizing of the New Testament, and accordingly he deliberately pursues his studies of early Christology right through from the first century to the time of Irenaeus. His attitude to the resurrection of Jesus is typical. He is concerned at one point with the origin of the idea of 'the third day' as attested in 1 Corinthians 15:4. He writes: 'Since for a critical consideration of the resurrection tradition in Paul any explanation of that three-day time lapse in terms of some event already known to the apostle which may have happened on Easter Sunday is ruled out, we are confronted with the problem of finding another derivation of this assertion.'[5]

What sort of derivation is to be looked for in this and other aspects of New Testament teaching? Here we come to the main aspect of Bousset's method of study. He belonged to the 'history-of-religions' school of thought *(die religionsgeschichtliche Schule)*, which paid particular attention to the cultural environment of early Christianity and argued that most of its ideas could be explained in terms of derivation from ideas current in its environment. In general terms this is a reasonable working hypothesis. Many of the concepts in the New Testament, for example, have been taken over from the Old Testament, and it is necessary when we are examining any passage in the New Testament to look for passages in the Old Testament which may have influenced the writer to think and write in the way he did. In the same way it would be folly to neglect the impact of Judaism on the early church.[6] But the particular contribution of the history-of-religions school was to examine the pagan environment of early Christianity and to lay it heavily under contribution as the source of Christian religious ideas. Thus, to return to our earlier example, Bousset was prepared to find the origin of the Christian 'third day' motif in a borrowing from the pagan myth of the dying and rising god or from the folk belief that the soul remains in the corpse three days before leaving it.

Bousset applied this method to the study of Christology. An essential part of his argument was that between Jesus and Paul there stood not only the primitive Jewish church in Palestine but also the Hellenistic Gentile Christian communities in Antioch, Tarsus and Damascus. Thus when Paul received his Christianity he did not receive it direct from the first disciples of Jesus, but through the intermediary of Gentile Christians who were open to pagan influences and whose faith had already been moulded by them. In this way Bousset was able to explain how Paul, a Jew, could have assimilated the Hellenistic ideas which, according to Bousset, were to be found in his writings.

On the basis of these premises Bousset attempted to draw a historical sketch of the development of Christology. Although the main theme of the book is the growth of the cult of Jesus as Lord (Greek *kyrios*), it is concerned with Christology as a whole, with the titles applied to Jesus and with the general concept of his person found in the sources. Bousset begins with the faith of the primitive Christian community which was expressed in the title 'Son of man', a title which expressed above all the hope of the imminent parousia of Jesus. Jesus is seen from the point of view of apocalyptic; Jewish apocalyptic categories were used to describe him and were transformed in the process. Jesus himself, it should be noted, was not responsible for this view himself, and most of the uses of the title in the Gospels come from the early church. Consequently the picture of Jesus' ministry in the Gospels represents the reshaping of what was known about him by the early church in the light of this new faith. A study of the earliest documents, Mark and 'Q' (the hypothetical collection of sayings of Jesus used by Matthew and Luke), shows how they depicted Jesus in Messianic terms. Here Bousset draws upon the methods and conclusions of form criticism, for example, in explaining the miracle stories as fictional additions to the story inserted to glorify Jesus.

Then Bousset moves on to the work of the Gentile Christian community, and shows how the title of 'Lord' came into use here for the first time to express the significance of Jesus as the present Lord of the church like a cultic deity in a pagan religion. Thus the effect of the use of the title was to transfer the significance of Jesus from the future (as the coming Son of man) to the present (as the reigning Lord of the church).

When we move on to Paul we find that for him Christ is above all a spiritual power with whom he can enjoy a mystical relationship; he has become the Lord who governs the entire personal life of the believer. This too is to be explained out of influences from pagan religions, but the development of this theme is too detailed to be capable of summary here. Finally, attention is devoted to John, in whose Gospel the earthly life of Jesus is now portrayed in the light of the Hellenistic beliefs about his person and mysticism is carried further as new elements are added from Alexandrian sources.

It would go beyond our scope here to pursue further Bousset's discussions of Gnosticism and second-century Christianity, although for a full understanding of his teaching this part of his book cannot be omitted. But our purpose is not so much to cite detailed conclusions as to examine the broad type of approach and its consequences, and this has already become reasonably apparent. In Bousset we have a strictly historical approach to Christology, one which attempts to trace logical developments in thought and to account for them in terms of known influences without recourse to the supernatural. Bousset's influence on Christology has been lasting. Unfortunately this means that his errors have also been lasting. His antisupernaturalistic bias means that his view of the history is one-sided and erroneous. His appeal to religious parallels outside Judaism easily turns parallels into influences, and much of the detailed reconstruction of myths that have been held to influence the early church has been shown to rest on a misreading of the sources.[7] Finally, his attempt to distance Paul from Jesus by means of a hypothetical Gentile church acting as intermediary must be pronounced a failure.[8]

## A. E. J. Rawlinson

Sixty years after Liddon's series another set of lectures on the Bampton foundation was devoted to the same theme of *The New Testament Doctrine of the Christ* (published in 1929). The author, A. E. J. Rawlinson (1884-1960), later to become Bishop of Derby, stood in the generally conservative tradition of British scholarship and saw it as his task 'to grapple constructively . . . with the work of Bousset'. In the course of the lectures he proceeds to criticize strongly the approach of the history-of-religions school. If that approach is correct, the church must choose between Jesus as a simple teacher and the developed Christology of Paul; it cannot have both. But Rawlinson refuses to accept the dichotomy and protests against attempts to drive a wedge between Jesus and Christianity. His answer to the approach of Bousset is to point to the basically Old Testament and Jewish influences which are to be found throughout the New Testament and thus to claim that there is a basic continuity between Jesus and the thought of the early church.

Rawlinson cannot be compared as a scholar with Bousset; nevertheless, he engages in a running fight with him and moves carefully along the course charted by Bousset via the Jewish Christian church and the Gentile Christian mission (note the significance of the word 'mission') to Paul. Rawlinson emphasizes the essential Jewishness of Paul and the Jewish origins of his thought. He rightly sees that the gospel had to be made available in terms intelligible to Gentiles, and that involved in this process was the risk that the gospel might lose its character. But he claims that this did not in fact happen and that the basically Jewish religious faith in God is visible throughout the process. From the very beginning Jesus was the object of faith. There is also an insistence on monotheism which leads ultimately to the Nicene form of creed. Throughout, too, there is the affirmation that Jesus is of absolute and ultimate significance as the Saviour of the world. At various points Bousset's detailed arguments are attacked and shown to be wanting; possibly the most important section in the book is the appendix in which Rawlinson justifiably claims that 'The phrase *Marana tha* is in fact the Achilles' heel of the theory of Bousset' and shows what desperate measures Bousset must employ to avoid the clear implication of this phrase that the title 'Lord' did not originate in the Gentile church.[9]

Rawlinson's work is important, not only because it is one of the few attempts to give a comprehensive account of New Testament Christology, but also because it shows that an orthodox understanding of the person of Christ can be reached by means of the historico-critical method which the author explicitly espouses. It cannot, however, compete in point of detail with Bousset, and therefore it leaves numerous questions open to further discussion. Subsequent research, however, has shown that much of Rawlinson's argumentation is sound.

## V. Taylor

It is a moot point which of our next two books should be placed prior to the other, since each was written independently of the other and each contains material delivered orally as lectures around 1955. But it may be convenient to consider first the contribution of Vincent Taylor (1887-1968). It is fortunate that the Speaker's Lectures in Oxford are not confined (like the Bampton Lectures) to a person who has 'taken the degree of Master of Arts at least, in one of the two Universities of Oxford or Cambridge'. Taylor was a Methodist minister who was largely self-taught and took a series of London degrees in theology in his spare time; he came to his study of Christology after a series of careful studies in Gospel origins, a trilogy on the atonement and what is still the finest English commentary on the Gospel of Mark. Thus equipped, he produced the lectures on which he based his trilogy, *The Names of Jesus* (1953), *The Life and Ministry of Jesus* (1954) and finally *The Person of Christ in New Testament Teaching* (1958).

We are particularly interested in this last work, but it is worth observing that the three books between them cover several different ways in which Christology can be approached.

In *The Names of Jesus* Taylor adopted the method of considering in turn the various Christological titles in the New Testament and evaluating their significance. In *The Life and Ministry of Jesus* he makes an attempt at historical reconstruction of the earthly life of Jesus, and thereby lays a foundation in Jesus' own teaching for the Christological edifice erected by the early church. Then in *The Person of Christ* he combines two approaches to the subject. In the first part of the book he works exegetically, examining in turn each of the main New Testament writers so that their distinctive contributions stand out. Although this task is carried out concisely, it is a good example of the redaction-critical approach to the New Testament, and demonstrates that the credit for the introduction of this contemporary method of study should not be given exclusively to German scholars such as G. Bornkamm, H. Conzelmann and W. Marxsen. In the second part of his book Taylor then attempts a chronological discussion of the material (such as was followed by his three predecessors) in order to see how the Christian understanding of Jesus developed and grew. By this combination of methods Taylor aimed to avoid the weaknesses of each, the tendency to view the material without reference to chronological development, and the tendency to group the evidence according to the interpreter's personal reconstruction. In the light of this discussion Taylor finally discusses the theological doctrine which may be built on the basis of the New Testament and commends a form of the 'kenosis' theory in which during the earthly life of Jesus his divine attributes of omniscience, omnipotence and omnipresence were hidden rather than apparent and active.

Taylor's work is important for its positive conclusions. He firmly holds to Jesus' consciousness of divine Sonship. Then he shows the strengths and limitations of the Christology of the primitive church which accepted Jesus as Lord but failed to relate its ideas of his person sufficiently to the doctrine of his work and the doctrine of God. It was left to the great New Testament writers to work out the implications of the Lordship of Jesus in these two directions and so to arrive at a more satisfactory understanding of his person.

Taylor's work is the mature expression of the views of a

great scholar who had wrestled with the whole Christological debate. Its weakness in the light of subsequent study is its failure to deal adequately with the period between the resurrection and the earliest extant documents; this was the period during which, on Bousset's view, the radical effects of Hellenization were seen, and Taylor does not probe into it with sufficient care. There is also a certain lack of precision and attention to detail in the discussion generally; we are afforded good summaries of the teaching of the New Testament documents, but there is not enough of the detailed evidence on which such summaries must rest. Perhaps this is due to the origin of the book in a series of semi-popular lectures; in any case it is a pity that Taylor could not investigate the material as deeply as he did in his study of the atonement in *Jesus and His Sacrifice* or in his commentary on Mark.

## O. Cullmann

With the lectures of Cullmann, which appeared in 1957 as *Die Christologie des Neuen Testaments* (English translation, *The Christology of the New Testament*, 1959), we come to the major work of a distinguished French scholar. The world of New Testament scholarship today is largely dominated by the influence of R. Bultmann and his pupils; it is characterized by a radical historical criticism of the sources in which the form criticism of Bultmann himself has been succeeded by the traditio-historical criticism and redaction-criticism of his successors, and by an understanding of the New Testament as the vehicle of a message (the kerygma) which must be understood in existential terms. The principal alternative to this global view of the New Testament has been offered by O. Cullmann, who has developed the concept of 'salvation history' (*Heilsgeschichte*) as the key to its interpretation. Cullmann fully accepts the historical-critical methods of his opponents, although in his hands they yield much more positive results; it would be a profitable exercise to discover why this is so. But the main difference is that he insists that the Bible bears witness to historical events which are the saving acts of God occurring in a definite sequence and leading up to the coming of Jesus as the centre-point in time. Salvation is achieved by what God does in history, and not simply by acceptance of a message which is independent of history and which frees man for 'real living', or, as M. Heidegger more philosophically puts it, for 'authentic existence'. These points were formulated in *Christ and Time* (1951) and given an exegetical basis and development in *Salvation in History* (1967).

But our interest here is in Christology.[10] Cullmann's book proceeds on the basis of the ten main titles which he finds in the New Testament, and he groups these according as they refer essentially to the earthly work of Jesus (Prophet, suffering Servant, high Priest), his future work (Messiah, Son of man), his present work (Lord, Saviour) or his pre-existence (Word, Son of God, God). This is not meant to be a chronological order of development, but within each section the material is investigated chronologically—its background, the possible use of it by Jesus, and the use by the early church. On the basis of this study Cullmann attempts to give a survey of the development of Christological thought, although he fights shy of offering a doctrinal synthesis of the New Testament teaching. In much of his treatment Cullmann comes to conclusions similar to those of Taylor, but his book has the advantage of being a much more detailed study of the evidence. His particular insistence is that New Testament Christology was essentially functional rather than ontological; the titles express the significance of Jesus as a Saviour rather than his 'nature'. The Christological question arose out of the work of Jesus: what kind of person must Jesus have been in order to do what he actually did?

The detailed study of the various titles is of great value, and the conclusions reached are generally sound. Cullmann insists on the fact that Jesus himself laid the foundations of Christology by his work and his claims, although the latter were expressed with deliberate reserve. Only after his death and resurrection did his disciples get down to Christological development. In general the background of the titles is traced to the Old Testament, although in one or two places Cullmann is inclined to find influences from elsewhere; he thinks that speculations about an oriental 'heavenly man' may have affected New Testament teaching about the Son of man, and he suspects that a pagan myth of the Logos is reflected in the prologue to John. He is also prone to dubious historical conjectures, as when he finds a group of Hellenists in Acts 6-7 who can be linked backwards with the Qumran sect and the circles which produced 1 Enoch and forwards with the Ebionites; this is less than probable. But the strength of the book is that he is prepared to grapple with Bousset and his successors in depth, so that his work represents the first really major challenge to their handling of the evidence. He finds a basic unity in the New Testament presentation of Jesus, and this unity is explained in terms of 'salvation history': Christology arises out of meditation upon salvation history, and is not a mythological representation of the significance of a person, the mere *fact* of whose existence and death was the theme of the earliest Christian preaching.

## F. Hahn

It is not surprising that the name of Cullmann appears about as frequently as any other in the index of the next major work on our subject, *The Titles of Jesus in Christology* (1969; English translation of *Christologische Hoheitstitel: ihre Geschichte im frühen Christentum,* 1963). This solid book of over 400 pages is the work of Ferdinand Hahn, a pupil of G. Bornkamm, and must rank as the most important of recent works on Christology.[11] It shows the typical German quality of thoroughness, and whoever disagrees with its conclusions must discuss the evidence in equal detail; it will not do simply to quote Cullmann on the other side!

Hahn explicitly follows the method of Cullmann in approaching Christology by means of a study of the titles of Jesus, and he takes up in turn Son of man, Lord, Christ, Son of David and Son of God; in a series of appendices he also looks at the suffering Servant, the high Priest and the Prophet as possible Christological categories. His particular interest is in the early history of these titles before the fixation of the tradition in writing. He is, therefore, not particularly interested in the redactional tendencies shown by the Evangelists when they set down the tradition in the Gospels. Nor is he concerned to set out systematically the Christology of, say,

Paul or the writer to the Hebrews. His contribution lies in a thorough analysis of the earlier period.

It is here that his most distinctive piece of methodology is to be seen. We have noted how Bousset claimed that between Jesus and Paul there stood not only the Palestinian Jewish church but also the Gentile communities. Hahn refines this distinction by his claim that we have to reckon with three stages between Jesus and Paul. To some extent Hellenistic influence affected the church through Jewish channels, and therefore we should distinguish between the Palestinian Jewish church, the Hellenistic Jewish church and the Hellenistic Gentile church. The first of these was Aramaic-speaking and centred on Jerusalem. The second was Greek-speaking and used the Septuagint as its Bible; it was more open to Hellenistic (*i.e.* non-Jewish) ideas and stood close to the Judaism of the Dispersion. The third was Gentile and Greek-speaking, and much more influenced by pagan concepts. Hahn is careful to observe that no rigid geographical divisions can be drawn which will correspond to this conceptual scheme; the criterion for distinguishing one area from another is the degree of Jewish or non-Jewish influence. Nevertheless, he believes that in this scheme he has a framework against which the development of Christology can be studied, so that the changes in meaning and use of a given title can be traced as it travels through the various stages in the early church. He thus attempts to repeat the work of Bousset in a more refined manner.

On the basis of this methodology Hahn works out his distinctive thesis that the various titles applied to Jesus were in general used at first to describe his role as the coming one (*i.e.* with reference to the parousia) and only later with regard to his exaltation and resurrection; in order to maintain this thesis Hahn has to argue that the exaltation of Jesus was not envisaged in the earliest Christology: after his resurrection he was regarded as being inactive until he should come again. Hence a title like 'Lord' was originally used to indicate the role of Jesus as the coming Judge. It was the Hellenistic Jewish church which first applied the titles of Lord and Christ to the risen Jesus and thereby began to ascribe to him a present role as the exalted Lord, seated at God's right hand. Finally, it was the Hellenistic Gentile church which began to see in the title of 'Lord' an expression of the divinity of Jesus and to read back this status into his earthly career. The establishment of this thesis requires that such a text as Acts 2:34-36 derives from the Hellenistic Jewish church and not (as Acts says) from the Palestinian church in its early days. Considerable amounts of Gospel material must also be regarded as having been modified or even created at various degrees of remove from the historical ministry and teaching of Jesus.

The thesis which we have illustrated from the title 'Lord' is applied to the other titles. Thus 'Son of man', which in the teaching of Jesus referred to his expectation of an eschato-logical functionary other than himself, was quickly made a title of Jesus himself as the coming Judge; then at a later stage it was used to refer to various aspects of Jesus in his earthly ministry and to his suffering. Jesus himself rejected the Jewish concept of Messiahship and probably the very word, but after his death on a charge of being a pretender to the throne (*i.e.* a 'messiah') the title came to be applied to him by his followers, again with reference to his future activity as the Son of man who would reign at the parousia. Since the parousia failed to happen as quickly as had been expected, the church was forced to modify its ideas and the title came to be associated with the present exaltation of Jesus, associated with his Lordship, and eventually used to describe his earthly role. Hahn makes a distinction between the titles 'Son of God' and 'the Son'. He holds that the former was first applied to Jesus with reference to his eschatological appearance, and then to him as the exalted Lord; then Hellenistic Jewish Christians used it of the earthly Jesus. At first it was understood functionally, but later it began to be understood as a description of the person of Jesus and related to the ideas of pre-existence and the Spirit-conception of Jesus. The other form of the title, 'the Son', arose out of Jesus' way of speaking of God as his Father; and eventually the two originally separate designations were assimilated to each other.

## R. H. Fuller

Of all the books we have considered *The Foundations of New Testament Christology* (1965) is the best suited to be a textbook for the student; it is clearly written, well organized and not too burdened with detail. The author, who is a British scholar now teaching in the USA, dedicates his book to the memory of A. E. J. Rawlinson and also expresses his indebtedness to the work of Hahn which he was able to consult before its publication. These remarks indicate its pedigree in the spirit of an Anglican 'middle of the road' position and its willingness to learn from the Continent. In point of fact the author's conclusions are very close to those of Hahn, although he follows his own independent course and has new light to shed at many points.

Essentially Fuller operates with the same scheme of Christological development through three areas of thought in the early church, and his discussion is likewise geared to the titles applied to Jesus. But where Hahn treated each title in turn, and in each chapter discussed the background of the concept and then its use at the various stages of Christological thought, Fuller inverts the procedure. He begins with a discussion of the background, discussing in turn what Palestinian Judaism, Hellenistic Judaism and the Hellenistic Gentile world had to offer by way of conceptual material for the early church to use. Then he goes historically through the various stages of thought in the early church and discusses the use made of each title at each stage. This means that the student who wants to trace the history of, say, 'Lord', has to turn to the relevant sections in some half-dozen chapters, and may be in danger of losing the thread; at the same time, the method brings out the historical development of thought more clearly than Hahn's method. What one loses on the swings one gains on the roundabouts.

Fuller devotes a full chapter to the self-understanding of Jesus, in which he attempts to look historically at his words and deeds and his possible use of some of the titles. He concludes that Jesus understood his mission as one of eschatological prophecy and that he expected to be vindicated by the Son of man at the end of the world. But the significant fact about him was not that he defined his task as that of an eschatological prophet (in fact he did not do this), but that the saving action of God was present in him; it was this latter fact which was interpreted in the Christology of the early church.

Fuller finds that the three phases of thought in the early church were characterized in turn by a two-foci Christology (the earthly life of Jesus and his parousia); a two-stage Christology (earthly ministry and heavenly reign); and a three-stage Christology (pre-existence, incarnate life, heavenly reign). On this foundation the New Testament writers erected their more detailed theological superstructures, but essentially the foundations were laid in the pre-writing period, and so Fuller, like Hahn, does not extend his treatment to cover Paul and the other New Testament writers. He does, however, discuss briefly the problem of building on the foundations, and the question of transition from the essentially functional language of early Christology to an ontological understanding of the person of Jesus.

### The state of the discussion

One can only be conscious of the sheer inadequacy of a survey such as this to do justice either to the writers so summarily treated or to the vast number of other contributors who have discussed, often in minute detail, individual aspects of Christology, and whose work has been passed over in silence. Something more of the detail will appear in the pages that follow. But enough may have been said to indicate the kind of problems that are current today and to show the areas where question-marks remain and further work has to be done.

The concentration on the titles of Jesus in recent works lays the pattern that must be followed in this book if it is to provide a handbook to contemporary study. An attempt to provide our own reconstruction of the historical development of Christology, based on our understanding of the use of the various titles, can at best be a conclusion to such a survey. In fact, however, one of the conclusions which we shall reach is that the early history of the development of the church and its thought is so complex that any attempt at a synthetic view of early Christology would be both speculative and premature.

A second point which emerges from our survey is that interest is at present concentrated on the early so-called 'pre-Pauline' period [12] during which the main lines of Christological thought may be presumed to have developed. Inevitably, therefore, the centre of our concern here must be with the same period, although it must be stressed that the only way to understand this period is by a careful study of the written documents in the New Testament so that the traditions utilized by the writers may be separated from the use which has been made of them.

Third, much recent Christological thought has been conducted on the assumption of a three-stage development in this early period. The strength of the superstructure is very much dependent upon the strength of the foundation; the conclusions may arise from the choice of methodology, although it may be argued that at least to some extent the correctness of the methodology is demonstrated by its fruitfulness in reducing the material to a satisfying historical order. It follows that the methodology itself must be carefully tested, and that our verdict on it will have enormous implications for the study of the Christology itself.

Fourth, much of the discussion in writers from Bousset onwards has assumed, or concluded, that the Christological material in the Gospels reflects the thinking of the early church rather than of Jesus himself. In one way or another the use of almost every Christological title has been denied to him and at most it has been allowed that he may have used the term 'Son of man' to refer to a coming figure other than himself. Although R. Bultmann is prepared to concede that 'Jesus' call to decision implies a christology', [13] he will not allow that Jesus himself drew this implication, or rather that we can trace how Jesus thought of himself from the evidence in the Gospels. This must strike the reader as highly odd: how could Jesus adopt the position of the proclaimer of the kingdom of God and yet not determine his own relation to the kingdom? Here, therefore, is a conclusion which requires careful re-examination. Upon its validity there depends a very great deal, for if it is not true that Jesus refrained from expressing a Christology, then some at least of the earliest Christology goes back to his sayings and not simply to the creative genius of the early church; the implications for our estimate of what the early church was doing are highly significant.

Finally, there emerges the general question of the validity of the church's Christology. Were there different Christological conceptions in different communities and at different times? Was the imperfect replaced by the perfect, or was the later development a perversion of the earlier and simpler formulations? What is the status of Christological statements, especially when language used of pagan heroes or deities is applied to Jesus? We touch here upon the questions of continuity and mythology.

In what follows we shall attempt to clarify the question of methodology by looking first at the nature of the early church and then at the ministry of Jesus. The main body of our discussion will be based on the main Christological titles, and in conclusion we shall attempt, however briefly, to draw out the significance of the debate.

## NOTES

[1] I have taken up this theme in *I Believe in the Historical Jesus* (1977).

[2] For general surveys of New Testament scholarship in this period, see A. Schweitzer, *The Quest of the Historical Jesus* (1909); S. Neill, *The Interpretation of the New Testament, 1861–1961* (1964); W. G. Kümmel, *The New Testament: The History of the Investigation of its Problems* (1973) and *Das Neue Testament im 20 Jahrhundert: Ein Forschungs-Bericht* (1970).

[3] G. E. Lessing, *Sämmtliche Schriften* (1838–40), IX, p. 291; cited by H. P. Liddon, *The Divinity of our Lord and Saviour Jesus Christ* (1867), p. iv (my translation).

[4] For an assessment of his work see N. Perrin, 'Reflections on the Publication in English of Bousset's *Kyrios Christos*', *Exp.T* 82, 1970–71, pp. 340-342.

[5] W. Bousset, *Kyrios Christos* (Eng. Tr., 1970), .p. 58.

[6] We owe to W. Bousset what is still one of the standard treatments of Jewish religion: W. Bousset and H. Gressmann, *Die Religion des Judentums im späthellenistischen Zeitalter*[4] (1966).

[7] C. Colpe, *Die religionsgeschichtliche Schule* (1961).

[8] See below, chapter 2.

[9] A. E. J. Rawlinson, *The New Testament Doctrine of the Christ* (1929), pp. 231-237, quotation from p. 235.

[10] For a summary of Cullmann's book see V. Taylor, 'Professor Oscar Cullmann's "Die Christologie des Neuen Testaments"', *Exp.T* 70, 1958–59, pp. 136-140.

[11] See my summary, 'Professor Ferdinand Hahn's "Christologische Hoheitstitel"', *Exp.T* 78, 1966-67, pp. 212-215. Detailed criticism of Hahn's book has been offered by P. Vielhauer, 'Ein Weg zur neutestamentlichen Christologie?' in his *Aufsätze zum Neuen Testament* (1965; originally published in *Evangelische Theologie* 25, 1965, pp. 24-72); *cf.* his similar remarks in 'Zur Frage der christologischen Hoheitstitel', *Theologische Literaturzeitung* 90, 1965, cols. 569-588.

[12] 'Pre-Pauline' means of course 'pre-' the other New Testament writers as well. In other respects too this handy adjective is imprecise, since some of the oral developments that preceded Paul's later Epistles (*e.g.* the composition of the 'hymns' in Philippians and Colossians) may well have been still in process during the earlier part of Paul's literary career. With these caveats we may continue to use the term.

[13] R. Bultmann, *Theology of the New Testament* (1952), I, p. 43.

# 2 THE EARLY CHURCH

In his book entitled *The Church and Jesus* (1968) F. Gerald Downing draws attention to some of the difficulties which surround the attempt to discover what Jesus really was like. Many people think that if we can simply remove from the documents the elements that reflect the thought and practice of the early church we shall be left with evidence that points us to the unknown, historical Jesus. One of Downing's main points is that the 'historical early church' is about as much unknown to us as 'the historical Jesus'; what we know of both is refracted through the documents of a later period. There is, in short, 'a *prima facie* case for a quest for the historical primitive church(es)'.[1]

Although we may suspect that Downing is unnecessarily sceptical with regard to what we can know about both Jesus and the early church, there is no doubt that he is perfectly correct with regard to the question of method. He is right to draw attention, as others have done before him, to the circular method involved in form criticism; here it is claimed that the Gospel narratives have been framed to suit the *Sitz im Leben* ('life situation') of the early church, and that the nature of the *Sitz im Leben* can be deduced from the same material in the Gospels. In order to make progress we need to break out of this circle, and attempt to find some other criteria by which the nature of the church's *Sitz im Leben* can be described.[2] We need to know something about the church which transmitted and shaped the tradition before we can state how it did so.

It is obvious that these considerations, which apply to the whole problem of Christian origins, are especially important in the study of Christology. A large part of our material is contained in the Gospels. Does this go back to Jesus, or is it the product of the early church, or, more precisely, what are the relative shares of Jesus and the early church in the formation of the tradition? We shall be looking at this question with regard to the place of Jesus in the shaping of Christology in the next chapter. For the moment we are concerned with the question of the nature of the early church, and the problem is whether we have any means of knowing how the church is likely to have shaped the tradition other than by making deductions from the character of the tradition itself—a process which suffers from that very circularity which Downing has exposed.

Repeatedly in our introductory survey we became aware of an attempt to shed light on the problem of the early church by recourse to the theory of various stages of development in it, culminating in the three-part dissection of the early church by Hahn and Fuller. But can the early church be divided into three parts with as much ease as Caesar's Gaul or the average sermon? Downing himself is critical of the procedure. Writing of W. Kramer's use of this hypothesis he says: 'He needs to do much more than he has in that work to show persuasively how the early communities he posits created distinct theologies which Paul was then both willing and able to absorb. And he has to show how his hypothesis does greater justice to the material than one which allows more flexibility and interchange between perhaps admittedly diverse groups. The admission of diversity makes good sense; there is not yet room for dogmatizing about the forms the diversity of ideas took.'[3]

## An assured result of criticism?

We have already seen how the idea of divisions within the early church was utilized by Bousset. It was, however, W. Heitmüller who gave classic expression to the hypothesis in 1910 with his claim that Paul did not get his Christianity directly from the church at Jerusalem but from Jewish Christians in the

Diaspora, probably at Antioch. Their outlook was Hellenistic and their theology showed features absent from Jerusalem theology, such as the doctrine of an atonement by the death of Jesus which made his earthly life theologically insignificant and the introduction of the title 'Lord' to describe him.[4] So long as Bousset's work remained untranslated, the most influential English presentation of this hypothesis was in R. Bultmann's *Theology of the New Testament* (I, 1952; II, 1955), where the exposition of Paul's theology is preceded by two sections on 'The kerygma of the earliest church' and 'The kerygma of the Hellenistic church aside from Paul'; it was during this second stage that Gnostic influences were highly influential on the early church.

It was left to F. Hahn to take up some hints from Bultmann and M. Dibelius and propound the hypothesis that the Hellenistic church really consisted of two elements — Hellenistic Jews and Hellenistic Gentiles. Both of these groups used Greek, while the earliest church used Aramaic as its basic mode of expression, and both of them were open to cultural influences from the Hellenistic world (*i.e.* the world which fell heir to Greek philosophy and religion and many other influences from the countries in the Middle East which had formed part of the empire of Alexander the Great; the predominant characteristics of this world were thus pluralism of religions and philosophical outlook and syncretism between different types of religion). At the beginning of the present century scholars were drawing attention especially to the 'mystery' or esoteric religions which flourished in this world; today scholarly interest has shifted to the existence of Gnostic religions, a field of research pioneered by Bousset.

Hahn and others who accept this general framework stress that we are not to think of three different localities corresponding to the different types of church, nor of three chronological stages in the history of the church, although it is true to say that, broadly speaking, the three parts of the scheme correspond to Palestine, the Jewish Diaspora and the pagan world, and that historically the early church moved out from Palestine via the synagogues of the Diaspora to the pagan world. The important factor is rather the determination of the amount of Jewish and Hellenistic influence on any given text, and in terms of this analysis it may be assigned to one or other of the three stages of the development. Some texts and ideas can be seen to have arisen at one particular stage; others can be shown to have passed through more than one stage and to have been modified accordingly. For example, the material contained in the discourse source used by Matthew and Luke ('Q') is said to have passed through both Palestinian and Hellenistic stages of transmission.[5]

The claims made for the effectiveness of this method in analysing the material are so high that we may be tempted to conclude that it is an essential and reliable tool of scholarship. But enough doubt has been expressed by leading scholars to make us stop and ask whether it is so reliable after all. Thus W. G. Kümmel stresses that it is virtually impossible to distinguish between the theology of the Hellenistic Jewish and Gentile churches with the resources at our disposal; nor does he find it easy to distinguish between the thought of the earliest church and the Hellenistic church.[6] Similarly, O. Cullmann says: 'We must, then, completely discard the rigid scheme, Judaistic original church/Hellenistic Christianity. It is not possible to distinguish so sharply as is usually done between a theology of the Hellenistic Church and that of the original Church.'[7] But the most sharp attack was that directed against Bultmann's use of the Jewish/Hellenistic dichotomy by T. W. Manson, who accused him of 'the building of Hellenistic castles in the air' and of producing 'an imaginary picture of the beliefs and practices of a hypothetical Hellenistic community'.[8]

## Palestinian and Hellenistic Judaism
The basic flaw in the use of this critical tool is that it draws sharp boundaries where none existed; but if sharp boundaries cannot be drawn, it follows that the whole attempt to place the development of Christology in some kind of evolutionary framework is questionable from the outset. The attempted analysis is over-precise and it does not do justice to the sheer variety of outlooks in the various early churches.

Perhaps the weightiest argument against the existence of the alleged distinctions in the early church is the fact that such distinctions cannot be made within Judaism. In broad terms one can of course see a distinction between Palestinian Judaism and Diaspora Judaism, the former more traditional in outlook and the latter more open to cultural influence from its pagan environment. But no hard-and-fast distinction can be made between the two such as would permit us to say, 'This idea *must* have arisen in Palestine' or 'This concept *cannot* have developed in Palestine'. W. D. Davies had already made this point, but the scholarly world usually fails to get the message until it has been proclaimed in German, and now at last we owe to M. Hengel an exhaustive, one might almost dare to say exhausting, survey of *Judaism and Hellenism* (1974)[9] in which he demonstrates how Palestine itself had been subject to Hellenistic influences in the period up to 150 BC; the survey breaks off there, but the indications are that the process still continued right through into the New Testament period. The whole of Judaism at this time, says Hengel, must be characterized as *Hellenistic* Judaism, and he is not slow to draw the appropriate lesson for the study of Jewish Christianity. It is no longer permissible to use the mere presence or absence of Hellenistic ideas as a criterion for establishing the *geographical* origin of the literature or concepts in question. Likewise, we cannot assign various concepts to different cultures without drawing rigid lines where none exists. At most we can speak of the Old Testament or pagan *origins* of ideas and note the existence of different spheres of influence which may have had a greater or lesser effect on particular writers.

Even the distinction between Semitic and Greek-speaking groups is called in question by research in this area. It is increasingly evident that there was a considerable knowledge of Greek in Palestine itself, so that we cannot affirm that the earliest church must have spoken Aramaic (and Hebrew) and not used Greek.[10]

## Palestinian and Hellenistic Jewish Christianity

If the attempt to establish a rigid barrier between Palestinian and Hellenistic Judaism is unsuccessful, it is unlikely that we can attempt a similar hard-and-fast distinction between Palestinian and Hellenistic Jewish Christianity. A basis for such a distinction can be found in Acts 6:1 (cf. 9:29), where there is a contrast between two kinds of Jew in the early church in Jerusalem, 'Hebrews' and 'Hellenists'. It seems probable that some kind of linguistic and cultural difference is expressed by the use of this terminology, and the most plausible view is that the two terms refer respectively to groups who basically used Aramaic (or Hebrew) and Greek, especially in worship, and who were attached more to traditional Jewish or to wider Hellenistic ways of life and culture.[11] The indications are that the former group were of Palestinian origin, while the latter stemmed from the Dispersion. To this extent it is legitimate to see the existence of two groups in the early church, reflecting a similar division in Judaism.

But the qualifications which must be attached to this statement are weighty. To begin with, it is beyond question that the language and cultural differences were not absolute, with the result that the two groups were not necessarily separated from each other by clear-cut characteristics. Further, the terminology is used loosely. Paul appears to have used the term 'Hebrew' to include people whom Luke might have included among the Hellenists (2 Cor. 11:22; Phil. 3:5); Paul's usage does not seem to be based on any peculiarity of language but rather on Jewish descent and the adoption of Jewish customs. The question arises: how would Luke have classified Paul? He was found in the company of Hellenists (Acts 9:29) and had been born in the Diaspora, but his upbringing was a strict Pharisaic one in Jerusalem (Acts 22:3). Like Barnabas he seems to have been equally at home in two worlds. Thirdly, it should be observed that the Hellenists were at home in Jerusalem and belonged to the church there from a very early date. 'To get back to a stage at which there were *no* Greek-speaking Christians is a hopeless enterprise, if there is any truth in Acts vi. 1.'[12]

Fourthly, we need to ask whether there is any evidence that there were two groups in the early church with differing theological outlooks. We should not be surprised if there were differences in theology; in the earliest period of Christian history, when doctrine was being developed for the first time, there must inevitably have been variations in the speed and manner in which new ideas were promulgated and generally accepted. Different understandings of the significance of the Jewish law and the place of the Gentiles in the church were undoubtedly current, and the group around Stephen, whom Luke calls 'Hellenists', were more radical than the 'Hebrews' at this point. Whether such differences were also visible in Christology is a different question. In any case, the hypothesis of two distinct stages in Christological development with a Palestinian stage preceding a Jewish Hellenistic stage is ruled out of court by the evidence which shows that these two types of Christianity existed from the beginning in close juxtaposition to each other.

### Jewish and Gentile Christianity

From divisions among Jewish Christians we turn to ask whether we can trace significant doctrinal differences between Jewish and Gentile Christians. So far as the early period under discussion in concerned, the answer here can be a confident denial. It is very doubtful whether any purely Gentile churches existed in the period before the Pauline mission, and we know that Paul's churches were composed of both Jews and Gentiles. M. Hengel is right to criticize Bousset for in effect turning the mixed church at Antioch into a Gentile community.[13]

In fact the church's evangelism among Gentiles was carried on by teams which were largely Jewish but also contained Gentiles.[14] It is impossible, therefore, to speak of a Gentile church in the early New Testament period, and it is preferable to speak, with A. E. J. Rawlinson and R. H. Fuller, of the 'Hellenistic Gentile mission'. To be sure, the extension of the church's mission to the Gentiles will have broadened its theological outlook. Preaching to people who were not monotheists demanded argumentation that was not needed in trying to convert Jews and Jewish proselytes who believed in the one God. Terms that were intelligible to Jews, such as Son of man, were not the most suitable when speaking to Gentiles who had not read the book of Daniel. Any missionary worth his salt would use terms and concepts familiar to his hearers which could be used to re-express the Christian message, and the use of the term 'Lord', familiar in pagan ruler and mystery cults, to apply to the 'one Lord Jesus Christ' (1 Cor. 8:6) was an obvious development of this kind.

It is important, however, to underline that this evangelism was carried on by Jews, and that it followed a pattern already set by the Jewish proselytizing mission in both Palestine and the Diaspora. We are still moving within the Jewish Christian orbit, and all that we have established is that, as the Jewish Christian church began to move out to the Gentiles, it began to broaden its theological horizons. We still have not provided a tool for making an accurate distinction between Jewish and Gentile theology. Hahn's 'Hellenistic Gentile church' must be dismissed from consideration, but Fuller's 'Hellenistic Gentile mission' may still be significant. For we may ask whether there is not a distinction between this and other types of early Christianity.

### The problem of chronology

A basis for distinguishing between different types of Christology may be sought, finally, in a consideration of history and geography. Historically, the early church did not go immediately to the Gentiles, but the recognition that the gospel must be preached 'to all nations' was slow of acceptance. Further, it was not the church in Jerusalem but the church in Antioch which was responsible for the Gentile mission. May we not, therefore, distinguish two stages in early church history, the primitive church in Jerusalem (largely traditional-Jewish in outlook) and the more Hellenistic church in Antioch which sprang up later and was responsible for the Gentile mission? Do we not have here a basis for analysing Christology in terms of a two-stage development?

At this point the question of chronology becomes important. In general, the idea of a development of Christological ideas through three distinct stages is open to question in terms of the time available for the process. A period of no more than forty years separates the death of Jesus from the composition of the Gospel of Mark. More important is the fact that a fully-developed Christology is to be found in the earliest Epistles

of Paul. 1 Thessalonians can be fairly certainly dated to about
AD 50 and Galatians may well be earlier. This reduces the time
available for development to some twenty years, and probably
even less, since it is unlikely that Paul thought up his Christology on the spot at the time of writing the Epistles. No doubt
opinions can change fairly violently within even so short a
period — the case of the rise and fall of Nazi thinking in
Germany has been cited as a possible parallel — but the short
time available seems to rule out the gradual evolution of
doctrine through successive stages. In particular, the idea of a
Hellenistic church quite remote from the tradition of the
ministry of the earthly Jesus appears to be impossible.

If we now consider the relation of Jerusalem to Antioch,
the time during which the Palestinian church could independently evolve its ideas before 'handing them on' to Antioch is
even shorter. At the most, the Gentile mission in Antioch
dates from fifteen years after the crucifixion, and this period
should probably be considerably reduced. It becomes even
more improbable that there was a special Jerusalem theology
developed independently of a special Antioch theology,
especially since there were plenty of contacts between the
churches and, as we have seen, there were 'Hellenists' in
Jerusalem from the very beginning of the church.

During this early period there was certainly a very rapid
growth in Christological thinking — more fundamental development took place in this brief period than in the next
seven hundred years, according to M. Hengel, and the same
scholar draws attention to the highly significant influence of
the teaching, crucifixion and resurrection of Jesus on his
followers.[15] The period in which the church began the Gentile
mission, which Hengel is prepared to date no more than five
years after the crucifixion, was of fundamental importance
for the development of Christology, and all the major advances
have their roots in this period.

It follows that the three-stage scheme of development has
been shown to be an inexact means of plotting Christological
thought. Not only are the boundaries between the three areas
of thought too fluid, but the very existence of the third stage
at this early date has been called in question. The circular

nature of the argument becomes apparent when defenders of
the scheme claim that the place of a concept on the map is to
be determined by the amount of Hellenistic influence (as
compared with Palestinian influence) that it shows.[16] Such
an enquiry merely reveals whether the idea in question contains Jewish or pagan elements; it does nothing to 'place'
it in a scheme of development.

If this tool is unusable it is right that we should be called
upon to fashion a better one. It is doubtful whether this is
possible. In place of the alleged development we may be
tempted to suggest that New Testament Christology sprang
fully grown from the early church in Jerusalem and that
there was a minimum of basic development at later stages.
Such a view would be as faulty as the one which we have
opposed. Rather it is probable that the early situation was
extremely complex, and that there was a considerable variety
in Christological statement among the early Christian communities as they tried in different ways to draw out the
significance of Jesus. It has been pointed out in another
connection that scholars are loath to say 'We do not know';[17]
here, if anywhere, is a field where the sheer lack of evidence
must compel us to admit that we cannot trace in detail just
how early Christian thought developed.

The effect of these considerations is to put a very considerable question-mark against much of the argumentation
offered by Bousset, Hahn, Fuller and others who have tried
to force the New Testament evidence into a strait-jacket
into which it was not designed to fit. The way is thus open for
a fresh consideration of Christology in order to see whether
a different approach can lead to more probable results.

But before we can look at the work of the early church we
must further clear the ground by seeing whether it is possible
to speak of any influence from the teaching of Jesus himself
on the thinking of the early church.

# NOTES

[1] F. G. Downing, *The Church and Jesus* (1968), p. 23.

[2] F. G. Downing, *op. cit.*, pp. 52-54. *Cf.* R. P. C. Hanson,'The Enterprise of Emancipating Christian Belief from History', in A. T. Hanson (ed.), *Vindications* (1966).

[3] F. G. Downing, *op. cit.*, p. 42. The reference is to W. Kramer, *Christ, Lord, Son of God* (1966), pp.33f.

[4] W. Heitmüller, 'Zum Problem Paulus und Jesus', ZNW 13, 1912, pp. 320-337.

[5] R. H. Fuller, *The Foundations of New Testament Christology* (1965), p.18. This point is developed at length by S. Schulz, *Q — Die Spruchquelle der Evangelisten* (1972).

[6] W. G. Kümmel, *The Theology of the New Testament* (1974),pp. 105f., 118f.

[7] O. Cullmann, *The Christology of the New Testament* (1959), p. 323.

[8] T. W. Manson, review of Bultmann's work in *JTS* 50, 1949, pp. 202-206, quotations from p.203.

[9] Originally published as *Judentum und Hellenismus* (1969). *Cf.* W. D. Davies, *Paul and Rabbinic Judaism*[2] (1955), pp. 1-16, 354. See also G. Dix, *Jew and Greek* (1953). For fuller documentation and more detailed argumentation here and throughout this chapter see my article 'Palestinian and Hellenistic Christianity: Some Critical Comments', *NTS* 19, 1972-73, pp. 271-287.

[10] See, for example, J. N. Sevenster, *Do you know Greek?* (1967).

[11] *Cf.* F. F. Bruce, *The Book of the Acts* (1968), pp. 127f.; C. F. D. Moule, 'Once More, Who were the Hellenists?', *Exp.T* 70, 1958-59, pp. 100-102.

[12] C. H. Dodd, *According to the Scriptures* (1965), p. 118 n. 2.

[13] M. Hengel, 'Christologie und neutestamentliche Chronologie', in H. Baltensweiler and B. Reicke (eds.), *Neues Testament und Geschichte: Oscar Cullmann zum 70. Geburtstag* (1972), pp. 43-67, especially p. 50.

[14] E. E. Ellis, '"Those of the Circumcision" and the Early Christian Mission', *Studia Evangelica* IV, 1968, pp. 390-399.

[15] M. Hengel, *art. cit.*, pp. 63f.

[16] F. Hahn, *The Titles of Jesus in Christology* (1969), p. 12.

[17] M. D. Hooker, 'On Using the Wrong Tool', *Theology* 75, November 1972, pp. 570-581; *cf.* 'Christology and Methodology', *NTS* 17, 1970-71, pp. 480-487. Dr Hooker is concerned in these two articles with the limitations of the form-critical and traditio-critical methods and the over-confident conclusions drawn by some of their practitioners; her comments are very relevant to the theme of the next chapter.

# 3 DID JESUS HAVE A CHRISTOLOGY?

Although contemporary study of Christology has concentrated its attention on the various titles given to Jesus in the New Testament, many scholars are reluctant to admit that Jesus himself used any of these titles to describe his own person and functions. Such an attitude may spring from a rationalistic attitude to Jesus which refuses to allow that he could have identified himself with any of the 'Messianic' figures of Jewish thought. For example, John Knox (the American New Testament scholar, not the Scottish reformer) says bluntly, 'I, for one, simply cannot imagine a sane human being, of any historical period or culture, entertaining the thoughts about himself which the Gospels, as they stand, often attribute to him.'[1]

At a more objective level it is often argued that any statements in the Gospels which reflect the theology of the early church stand under suspicion of being creations of the early church rather than actual sayings of Jesus which the early church has taken over and endorsed. We must, therefore, discard them in any endeavour to find out what Jesus may indubitably have thought about himself. 'Traditio-historical criticism', says R. H. Fuller, 'eliminates from the authentic sayings of Jesus those which are paralleled in the Jewish tradition on the one hand (apocalyptic and Rabbinic) and those which reflect the faith, practice and situations of the post-Easter church as we know them from outside the gospels.'[2] The principle is not always applied as strictly as this formulation implies, but even so the suggestion is that we cannot have any certainty that Jesus used Christological titles to refer to himself.

We may well wonder whether this methodological objection to ascribing the use of any titles to Jesus is justified, and later in this chapter we shall have good reason to suggest that it is a false principle. In the meantime we may find it profitable to glance at another kind of approach. This is the way suggested by Hahn when he admits in his book that 'other material of tradition which is not connected with a designation of majesty can be Christologically significant'.[3] This is not an easy path to tread. With a title one knows where one is; there is an identifiable entity to be studied. With the more indirect hints of Christology it is far less easy to be certain that one has laid hold on anything definite and to trace it through a variety of contexts. There is also a greater possibility of subjective judgment affecting one's approach, and also the objective difficulty of deciding what are the Christological associations of any particular motif; for example, the motif of dominion could equally plausibly be linked with the Messiah, Son of man, Son of God or Servant.

### Jesus as a real man

A pioneer of the type of approach envisaged here was P. W. Schmiedel. In a famous article in the *Encyclopaedia Biblica* he attempted at one point to discover material which had been preserved in the Gospel tradition, although its purport ran counter to the outlook of the tradition itself. In this way he isolated a set of texts which he believed could form the foundation for a life of Jesus constructed on a firm scientific basis. Writing in the era of liberalism he laid his finger on texts which stood out against the early church's belief in the divinity of Jesus and by contrast emphasized his characteristics as a real man. These nine 'foundation-pillars for a truly scientific life of Jesus' were Mark 10:17f.; Matthew 12:31f.; Mark 3:21; 13:32; 15:34; 8:12; 6:5f.; 8:15; Matthew 11:5.[4] It would be interesting to discover which of these texts would survive the rigours of subsequent traditio-historical criticism, but the basic conclusion remains sound. The Gospels do testify to the real humanity of Jesus, but they do so in an indirect and incidental manner. For them the status of Jesus as a man was not a theme of interest but was taken for granted. Only when docetism became a danger at a later date did it become necessary to emphasize the real humanity of Jesus, and traces of such polemic are comparatively few in the New Testament.[5]

We need not linger over the indirect evidence for the humanity of Jesus. More important is the question of the status which Jesus may have claimed for himself. Can we isolate evidence for this from the claims made by the church for him in the light of his resurrection?

### Jesus' use of *amen* and *abba*

In the first volume of Kittel's *Theological Dictionary of the New Testament* H. Schlier wrote an article on the word *amen* and concluded as follows: 'The point of the Amen before Jesus' own sayings is rather to show that as such they are reliable and true, and that they are so as and because Jesus Himself in His Amen acknowledges them to be His own sayings and thus makes them valid. These sayings are of varied individual content, but they all have to do with the history of the kingdom of God bound up with His person. Thus in the Amen preceding the "I say to you" of Jesus we have the whole of Christology *in nuce*.'[6] What Schlier is here claiming, in somewhat exaggerated language perhaps, is that the manner of Jesus' sayings shows that he lays claim to an authority which does not need any outside justification. Moreover, his teaching is concerned with the kingdom of God, and so Jesus is claiming to speak authoritatively about God and his activity, an activity which furthermore is closely bound up with his own activity.

Schlier's brief study was confirmed by the investigations of J. Jeremias, who claimed that the linguistic usage of Jesus in this regard is unique, that the sayings in which *amen* figures are likely on other grounds to be authentic, and that consequently the occurrence of *amen* must be regarded as an indication of the presence of the *ipsissima vox* of Jesus. Moreover, states Jeremias, here we have something that is not merely linguistically new; there is a consciousness of majesty expressed in a claim to divine omnipotence.[7]

Two Continental scholars, V. Hasler and K. Berger, have recently made independent attempts to refute this argument. They try to show that the sayings introduced by *amen* are not authentic sayings of Jesus but must be ascribed to later prophets speaking in the name of Jesus in the early church. The word *amen* was used in the Old Testament to express response to what somebody else said; the new feature in the New Testament sayings is that it introduces sayings and stamps them as authoritative. Hasler and Berger attempt to find parallels to this new usage in Judaism (so that it would no longer be distinctive) and to explain how the usage could have arisen in the early church.[8] There are several flaws in these arguments, and it is safe to say that the case put forward by Jeremias remains intact. In this one word we do have an expression of a unique authority on the part of Jesus.[9]

In a number of places Jeremias has also drawn attention to the use of the word *abba* ('father') by Jesus (Mk. 14:36). He claims that the use of this Aramaic term, used in intimate family relationships, as a mode of addressing God is otherwise completely unattested in Jewish prayers, that it indicates an unparalleled degree of intimacy in approaching God, and that it is an authentic form of address used by Jesus to express his own deep relationship to God as his Father, a relationship into which he admitted his disciples who used it in their own prayers (Rom. 8:15; Gal. 4:6). A detailed investigation of the use of 'Father' by Jesus with reference to God ties in with this special usage and confirms Jeremias's conclusions.[10]

There has been a greater readiness among scholars to admit the validity of this argument. It has been questioned by H. Conzelmann, but his objections fail to stand up to scrutiny.[11] We may, therefore, with all due caution accept that in these two words *amen* and *abba* we have indirect indications of Jesus' consciousness of his unique position.

## Jesus and the law of Moses

Most modern writers are prepared to admit that Jesus showed a sense of personal authority, although its character and significance are disputed. The evidence has been briefly presented by E. Käsemann: 'All exegesis is agreed that the authenticity of the first, second and fourth antitheses in the Sermon on the Mount cannot be doubted. In fact, these words are among the most astonishing to be found anywhere in the Gospels. In their form, they elaborate the wording of the Torah as a rabbi interpreting the sense of the Scripture might have done. The determining factor, however, is that the words *ego de lego* (But I say) embody a claim to an authority which rivals and challenges that of Moses. But anyone who claims an authority rivalling and challenging Moses has *ipso facto* set himself above Moses; he has ceased to be a rabbi, for a rabbi's authority only comes to him as derived from Moses . . . . To this there are no Jewish parallels, nor indeed can there be. For the Jew who does what is done here has cut himself off from the community of Judaism — or else he brings the Messianic Torah and is therefore the Messiah. [12] Käsemann goes on to argue that by this claim Jesus demonstrates that he cannot be integrated into the background of the Jewish piety of his time. Nor is this the only evidence. He refers to Jesus' attitude to the Sabbath commandment and to the law of purification, and concludes, 'It is by this immediate assurance of knowing and proclaiming the will of God, which in him is combined with the direct and unsophisticated outlook of the teacher of wisdom and perhaps lies behind it, that Jesus is distinguished from the rabbis.' [13]

In the same way both G. Bornkamm and E. Fuchs find that an unusual significance is attached to the teaching and actions of Jesus. Fuchs in particular has observed that the action of Jesus in having table-fellowship with sinners was a sign of forgiveness to them, so that implicitly Jesus was acting in the stead of God. [14] Taking up some hints from Fuchs, J. J. Vincent has claimed that the parables constitute a self-revelation of Jesus as Son, Saviour, Servant and Lord. [15]

The point to be observed here is that even the application of radical methods of study to the Gospels leads to this unavoidable characteristic of the ministry of Jesus. Somehow or other, Jesus still manages to get through the most rigid critical barriers. We must, however, go on to ask whether this radical picture of Jesus rests on a correct reading of the sources, and also whether the evidence does not take us somewhat further.

We may begin by observing that the impression of authority given by Jesus was very real. In the Gospels he appears as one who possesses authority (*exousia*) and delegates it to his disciples. This concept is to be found in all the main streams of the Gospel tradition, and there is no reason to doubt that the idea is primitive. [16] The word 'authority' normally refers to the delegated power which a person has been given by a superior in order to do various things that are normally in the superior's own right and power. [17] Jesus spoke and acted in the way he did out of an implicit claim that God gave him the right to do so.

In itself, however, such authority need be no more than that of any prophet who believes that he speaks in God's name and acts at his command. Was Jesus conscious of more than this? Käsemann's argument is that Jesus felt capable of abrogating the law of Moses and thus claimed an implicit authority higher than that of Moses. But there are certain objections to this way of putting the matter.

Does Jesus in fact question the authority of Moses and assert his own point of view over that of the Old Testament? It would be strange if the Messiah were to take a stand over against Moses. There is a good case for the view that Jesus was essentially attacking the scribal interpretation of the written law and not the law itself. On the contrary, he was sharpening the demands of the law by making them depend on the inward attitude of the heart. Thus the antitheses drawn by Jesus in Matthew 5:21f., 27f., 33-37 and 43-48 simply strengthen the demands of Moses. [18] The saying about divorce in Matthew 5:31f., taken with the parallels in Mark 10:1-12 and Luke 16:18, puts an Old Testament law into its proper context, and interprets it not in terms of Jesus' own authority but in terms of Genesis 1. There remains Matthew 5:38-42, where Jesus forbids revenge, but this is not a case of repealing an Old Testament law, since the purpose of the law was not to command that revenge be taken, but rather to state the set limits allowed. [19]

Similar considerations apply elsewhere. C. E. B. Cranfield has argued persuasively that the example of plucking corn on the Sabbath does not represent an appeal against the Old

Testament law, but an appeal to what was allowed in the Old Testament itself, as shown in the case of David.[20] Likewise, the healings on the Sabbath were not a contradiction of the Old Testament law. The most difficult case is perhaps Jesus' attitude to the purity laws regarding food which he attacks in Mark 7:1-23, but here too what is primarily under consideration is the development of the Old Testament rules by the Pharisees, and Jesus is concerned that attention to these should not stand in the way of observance of fundamental moral principles taught in the Old Testament.[21] Jesus' teaching was thus in defiance of the scribal legislation, and his authority was used to reaffirm the essential will of God.

But despite the possibility of interpreting Jesus' teaching in this way, it is probable that he was also contrasting his own teaching with that of the Old Testament. R. J. Banks has argued with considerable force that in Matthew 5:17-20 Jesus was asserting that the literal validity of the law lasted until 'all is accomplished', i.e. until Jesus fulfilled it by his own action and teaching; it is in the law's transformation in the teaching of Jesus that its validity continues. The Mosaic legislation was thus provisional until the coming of Jesus; from now on it is his utterances, in which the will of God is expressed, which are authoritative.[22]

All this means that Käsemann's sharp formulation of the authority of Jesus over against that of Moses will not do. It rests on a false reading of the evidence. We can, however, restate the principle in a more acceptable manner. First, in the time of Jesus the law of Moses and the scribal interpretation of it were becoming so indissolubly united with each other that the attack of Jesus on the scribal law was seen as an attack on the authority of Moses which, it was claimed, lay behind it.[23] Thus in appearance at least Jesus was attacking the law of Moses, and the question of his authority arose for the Jews.

Second, Jesus did in fact claim to know the will of God which lay behind the law, and he spoke in authoritative fashion to declare its true intention.[24] In doing so, he made no claim to prophetic inspiration; no 'thus says the Lord' fell from his lips, but rather he spoke in terms of his own authority. He claimed the right to give the authoritative interpretation of the law, and he did so in a way that went beyond that of the prophets. He thus spoke as if he were God.

### The authority of Jesus

This implicit assumption of authority by Jesus can be seen in other areas also. He forgave sins, both by his spoken word (Mk. 2:5; Lk. 7:48) and also by his attitude in eating meals with sinners. We have here a fact about the conduct of Jesus which is beyond critical cavil. As Fuchs and others have rightly observed, the implication is that Jesus acted in the place of God. [25] To be sure, the point needs some defence. If any ordinary person in the time of Jesus had eaten with sinners, the normal and natural explanation would have been, not that he was acting in the place of God, but simply that he was a sinner himself; this is precisely what was said about Jesus: 'Behold, a glutton and a drunkard, a friend of tax collectors and sinners!' (Mt. 11:19; Lk. 7:34). It is only when the action is seen in the context of the other claims made by Jesus that the Christological conclusion can be drawn. The evidence is inter-locking, and it is the cumulative effect which is compelling.

Similarly, Jesus spoke authoritatively regarding the inclusion and exclusion of men from the kingdom of God. The fact that he did so is again beyond dispute. He laid down the conditions on which men would be accepted, and he stated what would keep them out. [26] But the important fact is that in this connection he laid the stress on the part which he personally played. He saw the signs of the presence or imminence of the kingdom in the signs which he himself performed (Mt. 12:28; Lk. 11:20). He made it clear that the condition for entry to the kingdom was discipleship. Response to Jesus was the qualification for entering the kingdom and receiving its benefits (Mt. 7:21; Lk. 12:32; 22:29f.; 23:42). The sayings which state that the way in which men respond to Jesus will determine the way in which the Son of man will treat them at the final judgment may also be noted in this context; despite the criticisms made by some radical scholars, they can be shown to be genuine. [27] Of special interest in this connection is Matthew 10:28, a saying which is free from the use of Christological titles but which clearly implies that loyalty to Jesus in the face of persecution is what decides whether a person is accepted by God on the day of judgment.[28]

Then there is the interesting fact, observed by C. F. D. Moule, that Jesus expected no successors.[29] Even if the Son of man were regarded as a different figure from Jesus in his own expectation, this would not alter the situation, since in this context the Son of man is associated with the final judgment and has no prior functions on earth.[30] There is certainly no indication that Jesus expected any earthly successor. Indeed, on radical premises, there would be no time for any such person to act before the swift arrival of the parousia. In this connection it should also be noted that Jesus appointed twelve disciples who in one saying are linked with the number of the twelve tribes (Mt. 19:28; Lk. 22:29f.).[31] It is significant that Jesus did not include himself in their number; they remained his disciples, and he occupied a position above them, even though he interpreted that position in terms of lowly service (Lk. 22:24-27; Mk. 10:42-45).

The significance of all this is that it points not merely to a sense of authority on the part of Jesus but to a position of uniqueness. He stands alone; he has no equals. It might be objected that this is precisely the picture of him that we might expect from Christian tradition, but in fact we have built our case above purely on material that passes radical criteria for authenticity, and we have not used the vast amount of corroborative evidence that can be gleaned from the areas of tradition that could be said to stand under suspicion when radical tests are applied.[32]

### The prophetic and Messianic role of Jesus

What, then, is the nature of this unique position which Jesus was conscious of occupying? We shall examine two different estimates that have been offered concerning it.

In his examination of the self-understanding of the historical Jesus R. H. Fuller draws attention to the kind of evidence that we have cited and offers as a preliminary conclusion: 'An examination of Jesus' words — his proclamation of the Reign of God, and his call for decision, his enunciation of God's demand, and his teaching about the nearness of God — and of his conduct — his calling men to follow him and his healings, his eating with publicans and sinners — forces upon us the conclusion that underlying his word and work is an implicit Christology. In Jesus as he understood himself, there is an immediate confrontation with "God's presence and his very self", offering judgment and salvation.'[33] Fuller then goes through the various Christological titles and finds little help in them in expressing the nature of this self-consciousness. But at the end he examines the evidence that Jesus thought of himself as a prophet, and he finds that 'Jesus does not identify himself *expressis verbis* with the eschatological prophet in any of the current forms of Jewish expectation. But he does interpret his mission in terms of eschatological prophecy'. Again, 'as eschatological prophet he was not merely announcing the future coming of salvation and judgment, but actually initiating it in his words and works. It is the unexpressed, implicit figure of the eschatological prophet which gives a unity to all of Jesus' historical activity, his proclamation, his teaching with *exousia* ("authority"), his healings and exorcisms, his conduct in eating with outcasts, and finally his death in fulfilment of his prophetic mission. Take the implied self-understanding of his role in terms of the eschatological prophet away, and the whole ministry falls into a series of unrelated, if not meaningless fragments.'[34]

The term 'eschatological' is a notoriously slippery customer, but in its present context it refers to a prophet who announces the coming of the end, and who occupies a unique role as the one who helps to bring about God's final action in judgment and salvation. Fuller's claim that Jesus implicitly understood himself and his mission in these terms appears to be justified.

A somewhat different estimate of Jesus' role is offered by O. Betz. He has drawn attention to the way in which a number of traits in the ministry of Jesus are 'Messianic' in the strict sense. That is to say, they are traits which would be expected in the Davidic Messiah and not in anybody else.[35] Not all of these points are entirely convincing, but cumulatively they offer a strong case. First, building on the prophecy of Nathan in 2 Samuel 7, which we know from Qumran evidence to have been interpreted Messianically by at least some Jews, Betz argues that the confession of Jesus at his trial and his claim to rebuild the Temple constituted a claim to Messiahship. Second, the preaching of repentance and the authoritative proclamation of the kingdom are held to be the work of the Messiah. Third, the miracles of healing, especially the exorcisms, are the work of the Messiah in his capacity as a Saviour. Fourth, the attested Davidic descent of Jesus and his entry into Jerusalem fit in with the fact that the Messiah could be enthroned only in Jerusalem. And, fifth, Betz claims that the suffering of Jesus can be fitted into this picture, since suffering by the righteous must precede the coming of the kingdom.

There is sufficient evidence here to show that at least some aspects of the ministry of Jesus cannot be described as other than Messianic.[36] Moreover, says Betz, we are faced by the question as to how the early church came to regard Jesus as the Messiah if he himself had done nothing or made no claims that implied that he occupied the role of the Messiah. There is no satisfactory answer to this question if Betz's solution is rejected.[37]

But this means that we have now established two different and valid approaches to the question of who Jesus was. For Fuller he is the eschatological prophet, for Betz he is the Messiah. Can these two approaches be reconciled?

An answer may be found by examining more carefully the category of the eschatological prophet. Fuller does this in his book and notes that the Jewish expectation took two forms.[38] On the one hand, there was the hope of the coming of Elijah, or of a figure like Elijah, whose task was essentially to announce the coming of the end and to prepare men for it. In general, this figure was not regarded as Messianic, i.e. he was not the final agent of God in establishing his rule.[39] On the other hand, there was an expectation of a prophet like Moses, based on Deuteronomy 18:15ff. and attested in the Qumran scrolls (1QS 9:11; 4QTest 1-8). This prophet was expected to perform Messianic functions, performing miraculous signs, and restoring the paradisial conditions of the wilderness period.[40] This figure was that of an independent actor, not identified with the Davidic Messiah, in Qumran expectations. But the way was open for the prophet like Moses to be equated with the Messiah, and in effect this happened in rabbinic teaching.

More important is the view, noted by Fuller, that the suffering Servant in Second Isaiah was intended by the prophet to be identified with the eschatological prophet. It is extremely probable that the passage in Isaiah 61:1f., which is applied to Jesus in Luke 4:18f., was taken to be a reference to the Servant and was also understood Messianically. It follows from all this that the eschatological prophet like Moses, the suffering Servant and the Messiah were closely related to one another, and the evidence suggests that Jesus can have seen his role in terms of a fusion of these roles. According to Matthew 11:2-6 and Luke 7:18-23, John the Baptist asked whether Jesus was the coming one, a phrase which must refer to the Messiah, and received an answer in terms of the activities of the eschatological prophet. Hence it is plausible that for Jesus the eschatological prophet like Moses was tantamount to the Messiah, and with the establishment of this equation we are able to effect a synthesis between the views of Betz and Fuller. [41] Fuller's listing of the evidence is insufficiently explained by thinking of Jesus purely as a prophet, even the eschatological prophet; he fails to do justice to the use of 'Abba' (which he concedes is authentic) and to the further definitely Messianic motifs noted by Betz. [42]

### From non-titular to titular Christology
In our exposition so far we have taken pains to steer clear of any possible use of titles by Jesus, although we have looked briefly at such phrases as 'the prophet' and 'the coming one' which were used about Jesus. We have argued that Jesus was conscious of fulfilling a unique role without the need to show that he used any of the traditional titles in order to prove the point. But now this question of titles must be reconsidered. Let us return to the essay by E. Käsemann cited earlier. Having established the view that Jesus considered himself to be more than a prophet, but rather the one 'who brings with his Gospel the kingdom itself', Käsemann raises the question, 'Does this

mean that he understood himself to be the Messiah?' He replies, 'I personally am convinced that there can be no possible grounds for answering this question in the affirmative. I consider all passages in which any kind of Messianic prediction occurs to be kerygma shaped by the community.' He continues, 'But if this really was the case and Jesus never expressly laid claim to the Messiahship, it would be extraordinarily characteristic of him. He would have differentiated himself equally from late Jewish expectation and from the proclamation of his own community.'[43]

This is an extraordinary statement, at once unsatisfying and incredible. First, it is illogical. The question is raised: did Jesus consider himself to be the Messiah? It is answered negatively on the grounds that the Messianic predictions are not genuine. But this is to confuse what Jesus thought himself to be with what titles he used to describe himself in his public proclamation. These are two different things. For the whole force of Käsemann's argument, which we have tried to supplement and restate above, is that Jesus did think of himself as performing the functions of the Messiah. But it is impossible to see how the unique functions and person of the Messiah could have been separated in his thinking. The indirect approach to Christology demonstrates that Jesus spoke and acted as Messiah. The presence or absence of Messianic titles cannot alter this proof. Jesus could well have considered himself to be the Messiah, and yet not have used the title publicly. If so, the presence or absence of the title is irrelevant if other considerations show that he did think of himself as the Messiah. Käsemann, therefore, is illogical at this point, or he has, at the least, expressed himself very loosely.[44]

Second, Käsemann's statement is based on a circular argument. He says that if Jesus never laid claim to Messiahship this would be 'extraordinarily characteristic of him'. But how does Käsemann know what would be 'extraordinarily characteristic' of Jesus? He goes on to say, apparently in explanation of his statement: 'He would have differentiated himself equally from late Jewish expectation and from the proclamation of his own community.' That is a familiar statement, and we have already quoted a similar formulation by R. H. Fuller (see p.43).

It appeared earlier in Käsemann's essay, from which our citation is drawn, on 'The Problem of the Historical Jesus', and it expresses the so-called traditio-historical principle, according to which we can safely ascribe to the authentic teaching of Jesus only what cannot have been derived from Judaism or cannot be ascribed to primitive Christianity. [45] So what is happening is that this principle has been applied in order to discover what Jesus really taught, and then this has been discovered to be something that differentiates him from Judaism and the primitive church. One is reminded of the conjuring trick in which a rabbit is produced from an empty hat; to the best of my knowledge such a hat is never really empty, but has had the rabbit concealed in it at an earlier stage. So here Käsemann's conclusion has been concealed in the argument from the beginning as one of the premises.

Third, Käsemann's point is incredible. For if Jesus knew himself to occupy the role of eschatological prophet and Messiah in terms of the indirect evidence already cited, and if there is no positive reason to suppose that it was 'extraordinarily characteristic' of him to keep silence about it, then it becomes wildly improbable that the fact did not come to expression in some way in his teaching — if not to the public at large, at least to his closest followers. The early church certainly thought that he spoke about himself, as is shown by the direct statements which appear on his lips. But if it was characteristic of him not to say who he was, how did the early church come to the conclusion that he did make such statements? After all, the early church respected his silence on other matters, such as details about the coming of the Spirit and the atoning significance of his death; why, then, did they fail to do so on this matter? One is reminded of F. de Zulueta's comment on the probability that Pilate would have reported the execution of Jesus to the emperor: 'The probability of his having reported is not diminished by the fact that he is stated to have done so in Christian literature of the next century.'[46]

We have reached the conclusion that indirect Christology makes the existence of a direct Christology in the teaching of Jesus highly probable. The Messianic titles which appear in the Gospels need to be reassessed in the light of the fact that Jesus did know himself to be the Messiah. We can, therefore, in the remainder of our discussion allow for the possibility that the origins of the church's Christology lie in the use of Jesus' own Christology.

## The traditio-historical principle

Before we proceed, however, the general consequences of the discussion in this chapter should be clearly expressed. What we have done is to show that one part of the traditio-historical principle is self-refuting.

Let us go back again to Käsemann and his admission that the early Christians showed that they understood the distinctive nature of Jesus' mission by their response to him in terms of an acknowledgment of him as Messiah and Son of God.[47] If this is a correct response, and if it is highly probable that Jesus expressed his self-understanding explicitly, then the traditio-historical principle that what could be ascribed to the early church cannot be allowed to Jesus can no longer be upheld, since the effect of our enquiry has been to show that there was a real continuity and agreement between the proclamation of Jesus and the church's response to it.[48]

This form of the refutation will apply to those who uphold the traditio-historical principle in its most radical and least defensible form — namely that what is characteristic of the church *cannot* be allowed to Jesus.[49] If, however, the less radical stance is adopted — that what is characteristic of the early church cannot, *in the first instance at least*, be allowed to Jesus — then the argument can be restated: by strict application of the traditio-historical principle we have got past the stage of the 'first instance' to the point where it is necessary to go beyond the principle and take into account teaching ascribed to Jesus that is in accord with that of the early church.

Thus in both cases we have been able to show that the traditio-historical principle is self-refuting when it is actually applied to the Gospels. We can with a clear historical conscience return to a study of the Gospels based on the principle that only what can be shown to be incompatible with the general picture of the teaching of Jesus is to be disallowed to him.[50] To have been able to justify this method of approach is a great gain. It frees us from a most unreasonable fetter placed upon historical research, and at the same time it affords us a criterion by which we can evaluate the research of other scholars and see where their conclusions rest upon a false methodological principle rather than upon a false reading of the evidence.

## NOTES

[1]  J. Knox, *The Death of Christ* (1959), p.58.

[2]  R. H. Fuller, *The Foundations of New Testament Christology* (1965), p.18.

[3]  F. Hahn, *The Titles of Jesus in Christology* (1969), p. II; *cf.* the criticism of Hahn from the radical side by P. Vielhauer, *Aufsätze zum Neuen Testament* (1965), p.143.

[4]  P. W. Schmiedel, 'Gospels', in *Encyclopaedia Biblica* (1899-1903), II, cols. 1761-1898, especially cols. 1881-1883.

[5]  The evidence is so one-sided that it is possible for E. Käsemann (*The Testament of Jesus*, 1968) to argue that the Gospel of John, which is probably anti-docetic in intention, is itself docetic in outlook.

[6]  H. Schlier, *TDNT* I, pp. 335-338, quotation from p. 338.

[7]  J. Jeremias, 'Characteristics of the *ipsissima vox Jesu*', in *The Prayers of Jesus* (1967), pp. 108-115. It should be made clear that Jeremias does not consider all the sayings in which *amen* appears to be the authentic sayings of Jesus, but he maintains that there is a sufficient nucleus of authentic sayings to justify the statements in the text.

[8]  V. Hasler, *Amen* (1969); K. Berger, *Die Amen-Worte Jesu* (1970). See also J. C. G. Greig, 'Abba and Amen: Their Relevance to Christology', *Studia Evangelica* V, 1968, pp. 3-13.

[9]  Hasler's case is decidedly weak. *a*. He examines all the sayings of Jesus introduced by 'I say to you', the phrase which always accompanies *amen*, and draws the illogical conclusion that because some of this wider group of sayings are ascribed to others the *amen* sayings which are found only on Jesus' lips need not necessarily all have been spoken by him. *b*. He tends to assume the inauthenticity of the contents of the sayings introduced by *amen* without proof. *c*. He fails to see that the theological intention expressed in *amen*, which he ascribes to the Evangelists, could reflect the theological intention of Jesus himself. *d*. His attempt to show how the Hellenistic church derived its new use of *amen* to introduce statements from the responsive use in the Old Testament is unsuccessful. He fails to show that anybody other than Jesus used the word in a purely affirmatory manner to stress the truth of the following statement. Where *amen* is used elsewhere in the New Testament its effect is to confirm what has been said previously. *e*. Hasler makes the assumption that the early church did not distinguish between the sayings of the earthly Jesus and those of prophets speaking in his name. He even goes so far as to

claim that the Hellenistic church, as represented by Paul, has no need for the tradition of what the earthly Jesus said because its charismatic prophets could supply all the teaching that was needed. This assumption has been demonstrated to be false by F. Neugebauer, 'Geistsprüche und Jesuslogien', ZNW 53, 1962, pp. 218-228; D. Hill, 'On the Evidence for the Creative Role of Christian Prophets', NTS 20, 1973-74, pp. 262-274. Similar arguments are employed by K. Berger who has particularly tried to find parallels to the introductory use of amen in Jewish literature. Against attempts to find parallels to Jesus' usage see J. Jeremias, 'Zum nicht-responsorischen Amen', ZNW 64, 1973, pp. 122f.

[10] J. Jeremias, 'Abba', in The Prayers of Jesus (1967), pp. 11-65. The uniqueness of Jesus' image is not affected by the Jewish examples cited by G. Vermes, Jesus the Jew (1973), pp. 210f. (on which see J. Jeremias, New Testament Theology (1971), I, pp.61-68, especially pp. 65f.).

[11] H. Conzelmann, An Outline of the Theology of the New Testament (1969), pp. 103-105, argues: a. that abba need not denote an intimate relationship; b. that Jesus did not reserve the usage to himself, but invited other people to use it; c. that the distinction between 'my' Father and 'your' Father, which differentiates Jesus from other men in relation to God, is due to the early church and not to Jesus himself who spoke of God as 'your' Father to all his hearers.

The third of these arguments loses its force as a result of Conzelmann's own admission that the early church was in effect safeguarding what Jesus himself had really implied, namely that God is known as abba only to those who commit themselves to him in a relationship of trust. In any case, however, we may challenge the denial of the authenticity of certain texts on which Conzelmann rests his case. As for the second point, the preservation of the Aramaic word by the church is intelligible only if it was treasured as a word spoken by Jesus. It is sheer presumption that its use arose in the Aramaic-speaking church when all the tangible evidence speaks in favour of its use by Jesus. The early church knew that it was able to address God in this way because Jesus had invited his disciples to pray thus. While, therefore, the use of abba is not a unique prerogative of the Son of God, it is a privilege which Jesus alone gave to his disciples, and this fact implies his claim to unique authority. As for the linguistic point, Conzelmann claims that the use of the form 'my Father' by the rabbis was not essentially different from Jesus' use of abba, and that the use of pater (vocative) absolutely in 3 Maccabees 6:3, 8 indicates that the absolute form was in use. But if this reasoning is correct, it is inexplicable why the unusual form abba was preserved by the early church; if there was nothing to distinguish the usage of Jesus from that of contemporary Judaism, why did the early church especially remember the word he used? It may be granted that the absolute form pater was used in Diaspora Judaism, but Jeremias, who was well aware of this fact, claimed that this was in imitation of Hellenistic practice, and that there was no evidence of this usage in the Aramaic of Palestine. Nothing in Conzelmann's argument overturns the wealth of linguistic evidence adduced by Jeremias with respect to Aramaic usage.

[12] E. Käsemann, 'The Problem of the Historical Jesus', in Essays on New Testament Themes (1964), pp. 15-47, quotations from p.37.

[13] E. Käsemann, *op. cit.*, p. 42. Käsemann's argument has not gone unchallenged. H. Conzelmann (*op. cit.*, pp. 120-122) and H. Braun (*Spätjüdisch-häretischer und frühchristlicher Radikalismus* (1957), II, pp. 5f., 9) have denied that the form of the antitheses in Mt. 5:21-48 goes back to Jesus, or at least argued that it is questionable whether it does. They admit, however, that the content of some of the antithetical statements goes back to Jesus. Braun further argues that the authentic use of 'But I say to you' introduces sayings which do not radicalize the teaching of the law, and that the radicalizing does not go beyond what can be found in contemporary Judaism (Mt. 5:21f., 27f., 33ff.). The former assertion is incorrect; the latter is irrelevant in that it is the authority of Jesus to make the statements that is in question.

[14] E. Fuchs, *Studies of the Historical Jesus* (1964), p. 36; G. Bornkamm, *Jesus of Nazareth* (1960), p. 57. *Cf.* R. P. Martin, 'The New Quest of the Historical Jesus', in C. F. H. Henry (ed.), *Jesus of Nazareth: Saviour and Lord* (1966), pp. 25-45, especially pp. 31-34.

[15] J. J. Vincent, 'The Parables of Jesus as Self-Revelation', in *Studia Evangelica* I, 1959, pp. 79-99.

[16] Jesus has authority to exorcize demons (Mk. 1:27; 3:15; 6:7; *cf.* Lk. 10:19); to heal (Mt. 8:8f.; Lk. 7:7f.); to teach (Mk. 1:22; 11:28-33) and to forgive sins (Mk. 2:10).

[17] The word is used of God's absolute authority in Lk. 12:5.

[18] G. Barth, 'Matthew's Understanding of the Law', in G. Bornkamm, G. Barth and H. J. Held, *Tradition and Interpretation in Matthew* (1963), pp. 58-164, especially pp. 93-95; *cf* E. P. Blair, *Jesus in the Gospel of Matthew* (1960), p. 114.

[19] D. Daube, *The New Testament and Rabbinic Judaism* (1954), pp. 254-265.

[20] C. E. B. Cranfield, *St. Mark*[2] (1963), p. 115.

[21] The early church saw in the teaching of Jesus evidence that it was no longer necessary to observe the Old Testament food laws in a mixed church of Jews and Gentiles; it is unnecessary to assume that Jesus went so far as this; *cf.* W. L. Lane, *Commentary on the Gospel of Mark* (1974), p. 256.

[22] R.J. Banks, *Jesus and the Law in the Synoptic Tradition* (1975), pp. 203-226 (also published as an article in *JBL* 93, 1974, pp. 226-242).

[23] *Cf.* W. G. Kümmel, *Heilsgeschehen und Geschichte* (1965), pp. 1-14, 15-35, on the Jewish idea of tradition.

[24] Jesus was thus not formulating a new civil law, such as the law of Moses was intended to be; he was working on a different level, that of God's will for the personal and social lives of his people. *Cf.* R. J. Banks, *op. cit.* See also E. Lohse, *Die Einheit des Neuen Testaments* (1973), pp. 73-87. A very radical view of the authenticity of the material is found in K. Berger, *Die Gesetzesauslegung Jesu*, I (1972).

[25] E. Fuchs, *Studies of the Historical Jesus* (1964), pp. 20f.

[26] See, for example, Mk. 10:15 and the comments of E. Schweizer, *The Good News according to Mark* (1971), pp. 206f.

[27] The authenticity of Lk. 6:46 (par. Mt. 7:21) is admitted by R. Bultmann, *The History of the Synoptic Tradition*[2] (1968), pp. 128, 151, On Lk. 12:32 see J. Jeremias, *TDNT* VI, p. 501 and n. 20. The problems

associated with Lk. 22:29f. are complex, but see C. Colpe, *TDNT* VIII, pp. 447f., for a defence of a reconstructed form of the text. Our case, however, rests on wider evidence than these verses; it stands on the teaching of Jesus as a whole.

[28] I. H. Marshall, 'Uncomfortable Words VI. "Fear him who can destroy both soul and body in hell" (Mt. $10^{28}$. R.S.V.)', *Exp.T* 81, 1969-70, pp. 276-280.

[29] C. F. D. Moule, *The Phenomenon of the New Testament* (1967), pp. 68f.

[30] But in any case 'there is no scrap of evidence that Jesus expected one greater than himself to come and there is much evidence to the contrary' (C. E. B. Cranfield, *St. Mark*[2] (1963), p.274).

[31] The case against historicity is presented by P. Vielhauer, *Aufsätze zum Neuen Testament* (1965), pp. 68-71; for the other side see E. Schweizer, *The Good News according to Mark* (1971), pp. 127-129.

[32] It would obviously be impossible to present a set of evidence that would be accepted by *all* scholars; all that is claimed is that even radical scholarship generally accepts the authenticity of most of the material cited above.

[33] R. H. Fuller, *The Foundations of New Testament Christology* (1965), p. 106.

[34] *Ibid.*, pp. 129f.

[35] O. Betz, 'Die Frage nach dem messianischen Bewusstsein Jesu', *Nov.T* 6, 1963, pp. 20-48; *What do we know about Jesus?* (1968).

[36] The strongest of Betz's points is his use of 2 Samuel 7. It is not so clear that the motif of suffering must be associated especially with the Messiah.

[37] Betz discusses the suggestion of N. A. Dahl that the early Christians refashioned the false accusation made at the trial of Jesus into a confession of faith, and rightly rejects it (*What do we know about Jesus?*, p. 86).

[38] R. H. Fuller, *op. cit.*, pp. 46-48, 50-53. *Cf.* F. Hahn, *The Titles of Jesus in Christology* (1969), pp. 352-406.

[39] J. Jeremias, *TDNT* II, pp. 931f.

[40] G. Friedrich, *TDNT* VI, p. 847.

[41] For fuller details, see I. H. Marshall, *Luke: Historian and Theologian* (1970), pp. 125-128. Against the view presented here see R. Schnackenburg, 'Die Erwartung des "Propheten" nach dem Neuen Testament und den Qumran–Texten', *Studia Evangelica* I, 1959, pp. 622-639; W. Pannenberg, *Jesus: God and Man* (1970), p. 327.

[42] Attention should also be drawn to Jesus' conscious fulfilment of Old Testament prophecy; see R. T. France, *Jesus and the Old Testament* (1971).

[43] E. Käsemann, 'The Problem of the Historical Jesus', in *Essays on New Testament Themes* (1964), pp. 43f.

[44] Käsemann's argument becomes logical if the initial question is rephrased: 'Does this mean that Jesus spoke directly about himself as the Messiah?'

[45] E. Käsemann, *op. cit.*, p. 37.

[46] F. de Zulueta, 'Violation of Sepulture in Palestine at the Beginning of

62     THE ORIGINS OF NEW TESTAMENT CHRISTOLOGY

the Christian Era', *Journal of Roman Studies* 22, 1932, pp. 184-197, quotation from p. 195.

[47] E. Käsemann, *op. cit.*, p. 44.

[48] The other part of the traditio-historical principle has to do with the denial that what could have been said by any Jew of the time cannot be claimed as authentic teaching of Jesus — at least in the first instance. The untenability of this postulate has been sufficiently exposed by other writers who have pointed out the impossibility of trying to make what Jesus said possible against a Jewish background and yet not Jewish in content.

[49] The principle is stated in this radical form by R. H. Fuller, *The Foundations of New Testament Christology* (1965), p. 116.

[50] The position is of course more complicated than the statement in the text implies; that statement is meant to affirm an 'authentic until proved inauthentic' attitude over against the 'inauthentic until proved authentic' attitude. It is obvious enough that (on the assumption of Marcan priority) an alteration of a Marcan saying by Matthew or Luke (*e.g.* the variant forms of Mk. 9:1) cannot represent the *ipsissima verba* of Jesus unless there is reason to believe that the later Evangelists had access to another more reliable tradition. Again, if there were good reasons to suppose that a statement apparently attributed to Jesus (*e.g.* Mk. 10:12) was an addition by the early church in order to explain more fully what he meant (in this case, to provide a commentary on Mk. 10:11), we could not rule it out *a priori*. The point of mentioning these possibilities is to make clear that a conservative attitude to the criticism of the New Testament cannot exclude the possibility of finding material in the Gospels that is attributed to Jesus but does not stem directly from him in its present form.

# 4 WHO IS THIS SON OF MAN?

In the brief space at our disposal we must inevitably be selective in our choice of the Christological material in the New Testament which should be included in this survey. We have therefore had to leave aside any more detailed consideration of the theme of Jesus as a prophet, and we must pass over two other themes. One of these, which has been studied fairly adequately to date, is the understanding of Jesus in terms of divine Wisdom;[1] the other, which is in need of much further study, is the concept of Jesus as a 'divine man', a sort of 'superman' with magical powers.[2] Instead we must direct our attention to the phrase 'Son of man' whose importance may be gauged by the frequency of its occurrence (over fifty times, excluding parallel forms of the same sayings) in the Gospels.

The importance and difficulty of the phrase is further evidenced by the vast literature to which it has given rise. The field was surveyed by A. J. B. Higgins in 1959,[3] and then there followed a spate of further books and essays which justified another survey in 1966.[4] The following year saw the publication of six major discussions of the subject,[5] but since then the flood has considerably abated,[6] although there is no indication that satisfactory solutions have been found to the various aspects of the problem. Our attempt to survey the material will be especially sketchy.

## The Aramaic background
The phrase *ho huios tou anthrōpou*, literally 'the son of the

man', is something of an oddity in Greek, and we can be certain that it owes its origin to a Semitic phrase. The New Testament writers manifestly regarded it as a title of Jesus, but controversy has raged for more than seventy years over the question whether the original Semitic phrase could have been used as a title.[7] Old Testament Hebrew uses the phrase *ben-'adam* to refer to a particular person (*e.g.* Ezekiel, Ezk. 2:1 and frequently) or to mankind in general (*e.g.* Ps. 8:4). A corresponding set of phrases in Aramaic, *bar 'enash* and *bar 'enasha,* could be used to mean 'the man', 'a man', 'somebody' or 'mankind in general'. The phrase 'son of' in this type of formula simply means 'an individual member of the group', so that in effect 'son of man' simply means 'man', and we should understand that the figure seen in Daniel 7:13 was 'one like a man' or 'a human figure'.

So far the facts are undisputed. The controversy is over the two issues: *a.* Could a speaker use this phrase to refer to himself? *b.* Could the phrase be used as a sort of title, meaning the 'Man' (with a capital 'M', as it were)?

*a.* Although earlier scholars disputed the point, it has now been shown conclusively that the phrase could be used in certain contexts by a speaker to refer to himself.[8] According to G. Vermes, 'in most instances the sentence contains an allusion to humiliation, danger or death, but there are also examples where reference to the self in the third person is dictated by humility or modesty'.[9] But the precise significance of this statement is open to some doubt. Vermes himself apparently takes the phrase to mean 'I and nobody else'; it can be used to make statements which are true only in respect of the speaker.[10] Other scholars have held that the phrase refers to statements which are true of humanity in general and hence of the speaker in particular; it means 'I *qua* man'.[11] Clearly this uncertainty affects our understanding of sayings in the Gospels. If the phrase was being used purely as a circumlocution for 'I' in such a saying as 'the Son of man is lord even of the sabbath' (Mk. 2:28), does the saying mean that Jesus alone is lord of the sabbath, or that Jesus, inasmuch as he is a member of the human race, is lord of the sabbath? It is rash for one who is not familiar with Aramaic to pronounce a judgment, but my

impression of the texts cited by Vermes from Aramaic literature is that they support the second interpretation rather than
the first. If this is true, and if it is the only relevant consideration, it would make it unlikely that Jesus used the Aramaic
phrase to make statements that were exclusively true of
himself.

*b*. But the situation is complicated by the question whether
Jesus could have used the phrase as a kind of title. Vermes has
reiterated the fact that there is no example in Aramaic literature of the phrase being used as a title.[12] What about Daniel
7:13, we may immediately ask, for here we have the phrase
used in the Aramaic section of Daniel? But in this case the
phrase is being used as a description of a human figure and not
as a title. Vermes, however, is wrong, for C. Colpe has correct-
ly observed that against the background of Daniel 7:13 'son of
man' could be used to refer to the manlike figure described
there.[13] In an apocalyptic context people would realize that
'the Man' meant the figure described in Daniel 7. Hence it is
possible that Jesus could have used the term to refer to the
figure expected to come in view of the prophecy in Daniel
7:13; while at the same time the common use of the term in
a personal or generic sense *may* have enabled him to use the
term non-technically of himself as a representative human
being. If Jesus spoke about 'the Man' in ways that seemed
strange to hearers nurtured in the apocalyptic tradition, for
example, in terms of humiliation and suffering, it would not
be surprising if the hearers were thoroughly mystified and
asked, 'Who is this Son of man?' (Jn. 12:34).

### The origins of the phrase
But how would Jesus' hearers have understood the phrase?
We have spoken loosely of 'the apocalypic tradition', but
was there such a tradition?

There are only three places in Jewish literature where the
figure of the Son of man appears in an apocalypic context (Dn.
7; 4 Ezra 13; 1 Enoch 37-71). Before considering them we
should note briefly that the phrase does occur occasionally in
the Old Testament in a non-apocalyptic context. It is used in
Ezekiel by God when he addresses the prophet and suggests

his human weakness. It is also used in Psalms 8:4 and 80:17 where, it has been argued, it may have referred to the king as the representative man granted dominion by God (like Adam, the first man). [14] These verses may hint at something of the background of the term, although they have not exerted any direct influence on the development of the concept. [15]

In Daniel 7 the Son of man is a figure in a vision seen by Daniel which then receives an interpretation from a heavenly being. The manlike figure is interpreted as 'the saints of the Most High' who are to receive kingly power after the demise of the four kings represented in the vision by the four terrible monsters. In the present form of the book the 'saints of the Most High' must be the pious people of Israel, although it has been argued that originally the phrase referred to angelic beings. [16]

We must now distinguish carefully between the vision and its interpretation. The interpretation tells us what the imagery in the vision would have meant to later readers. But the imagery may have had a history and could have been open to more than one interpretation. We must take the history into account in understanding the interpretation given in Daniel 7:17f. According to M. D. Hooker the 'Son of man' is a symbol for the people of God; [17] the phrase thus refers to a collective entity, just as we may say that 'Britannia' symbolizes the British people. But, although this appears to be what the interpretation of the vision implies, it is exposed to the objection that the original vision seems to refer to a single individual and that the probable history of the figure points to it being the representation of an individual. We can square this history with the collective significance of the 'Son of man' in the interpretation by noting that a group of people can be represented by their leader. In certain circumstances, for example at a 'summit conference', the Prime Minister represents and in a sense 'embodies' the people of Britain, so that what he decides as their leader is in fact their decision. If the 'Son of man' is the leader of the 'saints of the Most High', he can properly be said to represent them, or even to 'be' them, an identification all the more easy to make in the ancient Semitic world where 'the one' and 'the many' were more closely

associated than in modern, western thinking.[18] This individual 'Messianic' interpretation of the 'Son of man' best suits
the nature of the description in Daniel 7.

It is confirmed by the subsequent use of the term in Jewish
writings, which shows that the original, 'individual' sense of
the term remained dominant, despite the possible suggestion
of a new, 'collective' interpretation in Daniel 7.

How far the ideas contained in these other writings can have
influenced New Testament thought is problematic. There is
general agreement that 4 Ezra, an apocalyptic writing which
uses the imagery of Daniel 7, was composed about the end of
the first century AD; clearly this document cannot have directly influenced Jesus, but the Son of man tradition which it
incorporates could have done so. The other Jewish document
which refers to the Son of man, this time quite extensively, is
1 Enoch, a conglomerate of apocalyptic visions and prophecies
of various dates. No portions of the detachable section, 1
Enoch 37-71 (known as the Similitudes of Enoch), which
contains the references in question, have been found among
the fragments of 1 Enoch in the Qumran finds; in this particular case the argument from silence (which could, of course, be
disproved at any moment by new finds) is a strong one, and
J. T. Milik has argued on this and other grounds that the
original edition of 1 Enoch did not contain the Similitudes.[19]
This would make the Similitudes post-Christian, but, even if
this is the case, they would of course still testify to the existence of a Son of man tradition which may have gone back to
New Testament times or earlier. The Similitudes show a
developed concept of the Son of man in which he has become
a glorious figure, invested with power to rule and to judge, and
attracting to himself some of the traits of the Messiah and the
Servant of Yahweh in the Old Testament.

What light can be shed on the nature of the Son of man as he
is presented in these texts? Two major attempts have been
made to account for the figure of the Son of man in terms of
ancient mythology. C. Colpe finds a background in the Canaa-
nite myth of the young god, Baal, who rides on the clouds to
the supreme god, El, the father of years.[20] F. H. Borsch
unearths a widespread myth about the First Man, the king of

the earth, which has left traces in various cultures and lies behind Jewish speculation about 'the Man'.[21] Common to both of these reconstructions is the concept of the Man as a heavenly or divine figure with royal traits. Both of them, however, remain speculative, and it is necessary for further work to be done in this area.

A somewhat different approach is taken by M. D. Hooker, who finds the basic background of the concept in the Old Testament itself. The Son of man is to be understood collectively of Israel as the heir of Adam. Destined to rule, the Son of man experiences loss of dominion and suffering, but will ultimately be vindicated by God.[22] There are difficulties with this collective interpretation of Daniel 7, but it is interesting that the link with Adam and his dominion over the earth is noted by this scholar also.

If the pre-history of the phrase is obscure, so also is the post-history. Was there a recognizable 'Son of man' figure in apocalyptic tradition? Both Colpe and Borsch hold that 'Son of man' speculations continued into New Testament times, so that Jesus and the early church could draw on a recognized complex of ideas. But this is a matter of inference rather than of evidence, and the gaps in the evidence have been exploited by N. Perrin, who argues that all that we have is a series of independent exegetical uses of Daniel 7 by the authors of 4 Ezra and 1 Enoch and the early church. In each case Daniel 7 itself provides the basis for subsequent thought about the Man figure.[23]    The differences between these scholars may be more apparent than real, representing variations in emphasis rather than in content, but Perrin's line of thought is carried to its limit by R. Leivestad in a provocatively entitled article, 'Exit the Apocalyptic Son of Man', in which he argues that 'Son of man' was *not* used as a title in Jewish literature, and that consequently Jesus was able to use it simply as a self-designation without any apocalyptic overtones.[24] This is in effect the same conclusion as was reached by G. Vermes working more from the linguistic point of view. What these scholars have shown is that it is very questionable whether there was a title, 'the Son of man' (or 'the Man'), which was common currency in Jewish apocalyptic circles. What remains, however, is Daniel 7 and examples of further development of the thought contained in it which suggest that the figure 'like a Man' in Daniel 7 had a fascination for Jewish thinkers and that allusions to 'the Man' might well lead the hearers to think of Daniel 7.

## The sayings in the Gospels

It has become customary to divide up the sayings in the Synoptic Gospels which contain the phrase 'the Son of man' into three groups according to their chronological reference; we may list them as follows:

> Group A: references to the present activity of the Son of man in his earthly ministry (e.g. Mk. 2:10, 28; Lk. 7:34; 9:58; 19:10).
> Group B: references to the suffering, death and resurrection of the Son of man (e.g. Mk. 8:31; 10:45; 14:21, 41).
> Group C: references to the future coming, exaltation and forensic activity of the Son of man (e.g. Mk. 8:38; 13:26; 14:62; Lk. 12:8f., 40; 17:22-30; 18:8; Mt. 10:23; 19:28).

This attempted division is not completely satisfactory, since we may well ask whether some sayings do not belong to more than one category (e.g. Mk. 8:38), but it is a convenient means of classifying the views of those scholars who in effect make use of it. We can then list the various approaches of these scholars by noting which types of saying they consider to be authentic teaching of Jesus:

a. The radical extreme, represented by P. Vielhauer, N. Perrin and others, holds that in every case 'Son of man' is used as a designation of Jesus and that this designation is entirely the work of the early church.[25] All uses of the title are due to the early church, although some of the sayings may be based on teaching by Jesus which did not originally contain the title. For Perrin, the basic text is Mark 13:26, which expresses the early church's hope of the future coming of Jesus; having interpreted his resurrection as an ascent to God (Dn. 7:13; Ps. 110), it began to hope for the coming of the Son of man (*cf.* Zc. 12:10ff.). From this beginning developed the subsequent application of the title to other aspects of Jesus' activity.

*b.* The conservative extreme is to attribute all the sayings in the Gospels to Jesus himself. Most scholars, however, who take a position at this end of the critical spectrum would express themselves more cautiously and claim simply that some sayings from all three Groups A, B and C are authentic utterances of Jesus about himself.[26] Among recent writers M. D. Hooker defends this position. In her book she considers the sayings in Mark in order and finds no difficulty in showing that sayings belonging to Groups A, B and C in turn could have been spoken by Jesus. He acts as Adam was originally intended to act with the authority of God on earth; his authority is denied by men, but he will be vindicated by God. This approach tends to play down the significance of the more apocalyptically coloured sayings, and it is not clear how Miss Hooker would deal with the larger corpus of sayings of this type (Group C) in the other Gospels. Nevertheless, it is important that she accepts the fact of influence from Daniel 7 upon Jesus; indeed, she even explains the suffering of the Son of man from the book of Daniel.[27]

Likewise, F. H. Borsch favours this position. We have already seen how he is able to attach a vast complex of traditional motifs to the Son of man figure, and in the light of this he does not find it difficult to show how the various facets of Jesus' teaching form some sort of unity around the figure of the Son of man. The trouble is that the postulated background is so comprehensive that almost anything could have been said about the Son of man by Jesus; one feels that Borsch's approach is not sufficiently rigorous.

*c.* Probably the most influential approach in recent study is that inspired by R. Bultmann and his pupil G. Bornkamm.[28] The latter especially drew attention to Luke 12:8f., a saying in which Jesus states that the attitude of men to *him* now will determine the treatment of them at the final judgment by the *Son of man.* Bornkamm insisted that here Jesus regarded the Son of man as a figure distinct from himself, and that sayings of this type alone had any claim to authenticity.

The early church naturally enough proceeded to equate Jesus with the Son of man, and hence there developed the other sayings in which Jesus is made to speak as though he himself was the Son of man. In other words, sayings in Group C, which refer to the future coming of a Son of man other than Jesus, are authentic. Sayings in Groups A and B which identify Jesus with the Son of man are creations by the early church.

Bornkamm's seminal idea was developed at length by H. E. Tödt, who placed particular stress on the way in which the term 'Son of man' was used to indicate the authority of Jesus.[29] Originally Jesus emphasized the authority of his own teaching by insisting that it would be ratified by the heavenly Son of man; later the early church attributed to him the authority of the Son of man himself.

Others writers have taken the same approach. F. Hahn and R. H. Fuller follow essentially the same lines.[30] So too does A. J. B. Higgins in his major book on the subject, although he suggests that Jesus expected that in the future he would perform 'Son of man' functions and thus paved the way for the church's explicit identification of him with the Son of man.[31]

In this same company too we find C. Colpe. His particular contribution at this point is to carry much further the attempt to write a history of the development of the concept in the early church. He allows some eight uses of the title to Jesus, all in Group C (Mt. 24:27, 37; Lk. 17:30; 21:36; 18:8; 22:69; Mt. 10:23; 24:30), and tries (most obscurely) to show how Jesus may have made a dynamic link between his own function and that of the coming Son of man. Then he goes on to show how the early church forged a static identification between Jesus and the Son of man, and carried over the title into other sayings of Jesus, including some (Mk. 2:10; Lk. 7:34; 9:58) which originally used the Aramaic phrase as a circumlocution for 'I', and others which were originally formulated as 'I' sayings (e.g. Mk. 10:45).[32]

d. A fourth approach leads to almost the opposite result from that achieved in the third approach. E. Schweizer has argued that it is sayings in Group A which in themselves have the greatest claims to authenticity with their picture of the Son of man as 'a man who lives a lowly life on earth, rejected, humiliated, handed over to his opponents, but eventually exalted by God and to be the chief witness in the last judgment'. [33]

Sayings in Groups B and C do not go back in their present form to Jesus, but Schweizer is apparently prepared to allow that some elements in them may be authentic. R. Leivestad apparently occupies a very similar position. For him 'Son of man' is 'nothing but a self-designation', [34] without apocalyptic undertones, and he is prepared to accept the authenticity of sayings free from the trend to apocalypticism which was found in the early church. This means that he is prepared to accept sayings from each of the three Groups. Finally, it is not surprising that G. Vermes fits in here also; for him sayings are genuine in which, first, Son of man is a circumlocution for 'I', and, second, there is no trace of influence from Daniel 7:13. [35]

## Principles of criticism

We have now isolated four main types of theory held in current scholarship, and must attempt to see whether we can formulate any principles which can be used to discriminate between them.

*a.* A basic principle is that the phrase 'Son of man' is found almost without exception on the lips of Jesus. The exceptions arise from allusions to what Jesus has said (Jn. 12:34; Acts 7:56) or to the Old Testament (Heb. 2:6; Rev. 14:14). This makes 'Son of man' unlike every other Christological title and carries two implications. First, it makes it most unlikely that it was used as a Christological confessional term in the early church. [36] There is no evidence outside the Gospels for the view that in the earliest church 'Son of man' was the key phrase in an intensive theological development. Second, it is overwhelmingly probable that Jesus himself did use the phrase; otherwise the fact that it occurs only on his lips becomes quite inexplicable, for we are then being asked to believe that the one person who is said to have used the phrase is the one person who cannot have used the phrase.

The effect of these considerations is to rule out the radical solution to the 'Son of man' problem. It is only fair to ask why the defenders of that solution have flown in the face of such a powerful argument. P. Vielhauer claims that it is because the concepts of the kingdom of God and the Son of man are not integrally linked in Jewish sources or in the teaching of Jesus; if Jesus spoke of the one, he cannot have spoken of the other, and Vielhauer assumes that he did preach about the kingdom.[37] But one has only to look at the conjunction of the Son of man and the idea of rule in Daniel 7:13f. and 1 Enoch 69:26-28 to see that the dilemma is a false one; we are not forced to drop' either element from Jesus' teaching.[38]

b. We observed earlier that there is no evidence that Jesus expected the coming of some 'Messianic' figure other than himself.[39] In view of our earlier discussion it would not be surprising if Jesus had appropriated some 'Messianic' phrase to refer to himself. The evidence that he was really speaking about somebody else rests solely on the alleged distinction found in Luke 12:8f. (cf. Mk. 8:38), Mark 14:62 and Matthew 19:28. None of these texts demands to be interpreted in this way, and it is clear that the early church did not think that they referred to somebody else, nor did it find them sufficiently ambiguous to need reformulation. Nor again is it conceivable that Jesus would place so much emphasis on the significance of a comparatively unknown figure in Jewish apocalyptic, when at other times he makes human destiny rest on men's response to himself. The defenders of this view have the utmost difficulty in explaining how Jesus visualized the relationship between himself and this shadowy figure, and they are compelled to reject the authenticity of the vast bulk of the Son of man sayings. But if, as we argued a moment ago, it is unlikely that the early church carried out a vast scheme of Christological thought utilizing the phrase 'Son of man' de novo, it is almost equally unconvincing to argue that they carried out a large-scale reinterpretation of the sayings of Jesus on the basis of a phrase that he himself used a mere handful of times. Thus the view that only Group C sayings refering to someone other than Jesus are authentic is implausible.

*c.* We can draw a distinction between what texts say about the Son of man and their use of the actual phrase. Colpe and Higgins, for example, are often prepared to allow that Jesus may have uttered a 'Son of man' saying without the use of that particular phrase: 'I am among you as one who serves' (Lk. 22:27) could be the authentic saying behind 'The Son of man came not to be served but to serve' (Mk. 10:45), and Luke 19:10 may have originally said something like 'I am come to seek and to save that which was lost'. J. Jeremias has elaborated this approach and proposed that in every case where we have two forms of a saying, one with 'Son of man' and one without it, the latter represents the more primitive form. [40]

Jeremias's argument is not convincing in this form. One cannot arbitrarily postulate general rules of this kind, and a number of his alleged pairs are not real parallels. Nevertheless, the approach leads to an important point. Once the offending phrase has been removed from the texts, it is often the case that there are no other serious grounds for attacking their authenticity. If so, we have a strong body of evidence containing the phrase to place over against the few texts cited by Tödt and others as evidence that Jesus used the phrase to refer to somebody else; if the only real evidence against the authenticity of this wider group of texts is simply that they use 'Son of man' to refer to Jesus, then we may well question the interpretation of Luke 12:8f. and the other texts as evidence that Jesus was not referring to himself. In this way the probability that Jesus did refer to himself by this phrase is greatly increased. [41]

*d.* Greater problems and uncertainties arise when we examine the sayings in the Gospels in the light of Jewish usage of the phrase 'Son of man'. There are some four different lines of approach here. First, there is the view that Jesus' usage must be seen entirely against the background of a non-titular use of the phrase as a circumlocution for 'I' or self-designation (R. Leivestad; G. Vermes). The weaknesses of this view are two in number. There is the dispute among the philologians whether 'Son of man' could be used to make statements which were true exclusively of the speaker. One or two sayings of

Jesus may originally have referred to man in general rather than exclusively to himself (Lk. 7:34; 9:58; 12:10; Mk. 2:28), but this explanation will not account for the other sayings. In the absence of clear evidence that 'Son of man' could be used as a plain circumlocution for 'I and no-one else', we do well to be cautious about explaining its use in this way. The other weakness of this view is that it postulates that Daniel 7:13 exerted little or no influence upon Jesus, and that apocalyptic uses of 'Son of man' are generally inauthentic; this is a quite arbitrary postulate.

Second, there is the view that the non-apocalyptic use of the phrase in the Old Testament (especially in Ezekiel) was the main influence upon Jesus (E. Schweizer). Acceptance of this view is again bound up with the thesis that use of Daniel 7 is to be traced to the early church rather than to Jesus. The influence of Ezekiel upon Jesus is worthy of further investigation, but again it is unnecessary to make an either/or between Ezekiel and Daniel.

Third, there is the theory of an apocalyptic tradition, partly visible in 4 Ezra and 1 Enoch, partly a matter of inference, which has influenced Jesus and the early church. Upholders of this view tend to regard the sayings in Group C as forming the basic nucleus in the collection, and to argue that in the genuine sayings Jesus is referring to someone other than himself. (A notable exception to this rule is J. Jeremias, who thinks that Jesus used the phrase to refer to himself in his future exaltation.[42]) We have already seen the difficulties involved in assuming the existence of this tradition, but the fact remains that the use of 'Son of man' in the Gospels is not altogether unlike the use in 4 Ezra and 1 Enoch. It seems likely that in these works we have some indication of how Jewish exegesis dealt with the Old Testament, and that they shed some light on the usage in the Gospels.

Fourth, there remains the influence of Daniel 7. We know that this chapter was used by the early church, and its influence is clear in sayings attributed to Jesus (Mk. 13:26; 14:62). The question is whether it is a sufficient background for all the sayings. The answer to this question is obviously 'no'. Attempts to derive the present humiliation and suffering of the Son of man as an earthly figure from Daniel 7 are not completely convincing. The apocalyptic tradition of exegesis leads us even further away from this concept of the Son of man.

It follows that no single source of influence is sufficient to explain the usage in the Gospels, and that some combination of influences must be postulated; there may also, of course, be other influences than those mentioned which may contribute to the formation of the sayings.

e. We are faced by a complex situation in which the phrase 'Son of man' is used in a variety of ways and cannot be accounted for solely in terms of one source of influence. Two main types of possibility now emerge. The one is that there was one original type of saying which formed the basis for a gradual development in the thought of the early church. We have already seen suggestions as to how the phrase may have been originally used of the coming eschatological figure; this figure was identified with Jesus, and then the title was increasingly used with reference to Jesus in his other, earthly roles. While the details of the process are not absolutely clear, there is the possibility of drawing up a 'tradition history' of the developing use of the phrase 'Son of man' by the early church. The other possibility is that one person (i.e. Jesus) was responsible for a creative synthesis in which the phrase was used in a variety of ways but with an inner principle of unity. These are the two main possibilities, but there is also the possibility of combining the two hypotheses — the seminal contribution was that of Jesus himself, but the early church carried the development of his ideas further.

The argument against the first of these two possibilities is that so far we have seen little evidence that the early church used the phrase 'Son of man' as a Christological title. Accordingly the question is whether the actual sayings in the Gospels demand this hypothesis. If there is some basic uniting principle to be found in the sayings, this will be more likely to have arisen in the mind of one person than as the result of a gradual evolution. Is there a basic common factor?

Such a common factor will not necessarily be a simple idea.

The complexity of the situation suggests that there would have to be a complex principle of unity — but not so complex that it makes the hypothesis of evolutionary development in the early church more probable.

We would suggest that the following considerations are relevant. First, throughout the sayings there runs the general thought of the authority of Jesus. The Son of man is a figure of authority on earth and will one day appear endowed with heavenly authority when he participates in the last judgment; yet his authority is spurned by men and it is only by the action of God that his authority is finally vindicated.[43] This theme of authority is the basic factor in the general corpus of sayings. It fits in with Jesus' own consciousness of authority which was explored in the previous chapter.

Second, throughout the sayings there can be traced the influence of Old Testament teaching, especially of Daniel 7 where the fundamental thought of authority, judgment and rule is expressed. Of particular importance is the way in which the career of the Son of man is expressed in terms of the suffering righteous one (E. Schweizer), a theme which has influenced Daniel and which is most fully expressed in the suffering Servant figure in Isaiah 40-55. Despite arguments to the contrary, it still remains most probable that the motif of the suffering Servant is expressed in the teaching of Jesus.[44] Now understanding of the person of Jesus in terms of Old Testament concepts is certainly characteristic of the early church, but the case that Jesus himself also thought in this way is overwhelmingly strong, and therefore it cannot be argued that the presence of Old Testament allusions in the Son of man sayings points to their origin in the early church.[45]

Third, it is unlikely that Jesus used the phrase in two quite separate ways, as a neutral self-designation and as a 'Messianic' title. If he used it as a self-designation, then the basis for this lay not so much in a possible Aramaic idiom as in an identification of himself with 'the Man' or 'the manlike Figure' in Daniel 7. But the way in which Jesus spoke of 'the Man' must have led to considerable lack of understanding on the part of his hearers, since he used the phrase in a non-apocalyptic manner to refer to his own present situation. Those who did not possess the key — the implicit reference to Daniel 7:13 — would be mystified by the usage. If this is the case, it follows that Jesus did not deliberately draw attention to his role but used a somewhat mysterious expression. But the term had associations with Adam as the first man and probably suggested a figure who came from God and was ideally fitted to be God's agent; it may have had associations with divine wisdom which was increasingly regarded as an independent hypostasis alongside God. These associations made the term an admirable one for expressing the authority of which Jesus was conscious.

It would require a detailed investigation of the various sayings to see how far this common factor serves to unite them. But there is at least a working hypothesis here which can account for many of the sayings. So far as historical investigation can take us, we have good reason to suppose that a nucleus of sayings of various types goes back to Jesus himself. This still leaves the question as to how far the early church used the phrase 'Son of man' creatively. This possibility can be explored in three directions. There is, first of all, the evidence that Paul and other teachers in the early church were familiar with the concept of Jesus as 'the Man' — the correct Greek equivalent of 'Son of man' — and this suggests that to some extent the early church was familiar with the motif, although its development is significantly different from the usage of Jesus and takes us into the area of Adam/Christ typology.[46] Second, there is the tradition of Jesus' sayings in the Gospel of John in which Jesus is presented much more definitely as a figure who has descended from heaven and will ascend to heaven. There are indications that this tradition has undergone some development, just as is the case with the other teaching of Jesus recorded in this Gospel.[47] Third, there is the evidence of the Synoptic Gospels themselves which indicate that the early church preserved the Son of man sayings. As late as the composition of the Gospels there was some redaction of the 'Son of man' sayings,[48] and the possibility of earlier activity of this kind cannot be ruled out; but the view that there was a creative reinterpretation of the person of Jesus in terms of the Son of man is not a very likely one.[49]

From our survey it is evident that there are no easy solutions to the 'Son of man' problem, and there is no consensus of opinion among scholars.[50] But it may be claimed that the view that Jesus spoke of himself by means of this phrase offers the least difficulties, and that here we have a valuable insight into his self-understanding.

## NOTES

[1] U. Wilckens and G. Fohrer, *TDNT* VII, pp. 465-526; M. J. Suggs, *Wisdom, Christology and Law in Matthew's Gospel* (1970); F. Christ, *Jesus Sophia* (1970); R. G. Hamerton-Kelly, *Pre-Existence, Wisdom and the Son of Man* (1973)

[2] H. D. Betz, 'Jesus as Divine Man', in F. T. Trotter (ed.), *Jesus and the Historian* (1968), pp. 114-133; J. M. Hull, *Hellenistic Magic and the Synoptic Tradition* (1974); M. Smith, 'Prolegomena to a Discussion of Aretalogies. Divine Men, the Gospels and Jesus', *JBL* 90, 1971, pp. 174-199; for a critique of this approach see O. Betz, 'The Concept of the so-called "Divine Man" in Mark's Christology', in D. E. Aune (ed.), *Studies in New Testament and Early Christian Literature* (1972), pp. 229-240; W. L. Lane, *'Theios Anēr* Christology and the Gospel of Mark', in R. N. Longenecker and M. C. Tenney (eds.), *New Dimensions in New Testament Study* (1974).

[3] A. J. B. Higgins, 'Son of man — *Forschung* since "The Teaching of Jesus"', in A. J. B. Higgins (ed.), *New Testament Essays: Studies in Memory of T. W. Manson* (1959), pp. 119-135. The reference in the title of the essay is to T. W. Manson's book of that name.

[4] I. H. Marshall, 'The Synoptic Son of Man Sayings in Recent Discussion', *NTS* 12, 1965-66, pp. 327-351. The present chapter is based to a large extent on this article and the one cited in the next footnote.

[5] N. Perrin, *Rediscovering the Teaching of Jesus* (1967); M. D. Hooker, *The Son of Man in Mark* (1967); C. K. Barrett, *Jesus and the Gospel Tradition* (1967); F. H. Borsch, *The Son of Man in Myth and History* (1967); C. Colpe in *TDNT* VIII, pp. 400-407; J. Jeremias, 'Die älteste Schicht der Menschensohn-Logien', *ZNW* 58, 1967, pp. 159-172 (summarized in *New Testament Theology* (1971), 1, pp. 257-276). See my survey, 'The Son of Man in Contemporary Debate', *EQ* 42, 1970, pp. 67-87.

[6] Recent works include: W. Marxsen, *The Beginnings of Christology: a Study of its Problems* (1969); F. H. Borsch, *The Christian and Gnostic Son of Man* (1970); R. Maddox, 'The Quest for Valid Methods in "Son of Man" Research', *TSFB* 61, Autumn 1971, pp. 14-21; R. Leivestad, 'Exit the Apocalyptic Son of Man', *NTS* 18, 1971-72, pp. 243-267; G. Vermes, *Jesus the Jew* (1973), pp. 160-191; N. Perrin, *A Modern Pilgrimage in New Testament Christology* (1974); *cf.* G. N. Stanton,

*Jesus of Nazareth in New Testament Preaching* (1974), pp. 156-165.
[7] This was denied by H. Lietzmann, *Der Menschensohn* (1896).
[8] G. Vermes, 'The Use of *bar nash/bar nasha* in Jewish Aramaic', Appendix E in M. Black, *An Aramaic Approach to the Gospels and Acts*[3] (1967), pp. 310-328. The article is summarized in G. Vermes, *Jesus the Jew* (1973).
[9] G. Vermes, *art. cit.*, p. 327.
[10] G. Vermes, *Jesus the Jew*, pp. 164-168, 189.
[11] J. Jeremias, *New Testament Theology* (1971), I, p. 261 n. 1; A. Gelston, 'A Sidelight on the "Son of Man' ", *SJT* 22, 1969, pp. 189-196. See further R. Le Déaut's review of Black's book in *Biblica* 50, 1968, pp. 388-399, especially pp. 397-399.
[12] G. Vermes, *Jesus the Jew*, pp. 169-177. For the equally negative evidence from the Qumran scrolls see J. A. Fitzmyer, 'The Contribution of Qumran Aramaic to the Study of the New Testament', *NTS* 20, 1973-74, pp. 382-407, especially pp. 396f.
[13] C. Colpe, *TDNT* VIII, p. 404.
[14] F. H. Borsch, *The Son of Man in Myth and History* (1967), pp. 114-117; D. Hill, '"Son of Man" in Psalm 80 v. 17', *Nov.T* 15, 1973, pp. 261-269. But this exegesis is not universally accepted; *cf.* C. Colpe, *TDNT* VIII, p. 407.
[15] When Ps. 8 is quoted in Heb. 2:6-8, the reference to the Son of man is not of primary importance.
[16] See the discussion and bibliography in M. D. Hooker, *The Son of Man in Mark* (1967), p. 13 n. 3.
[17] M. D. Hooker, *op. cit.*, pp. 11-30.
[18] *Cf.* A. R. Johnson, *The One and the Many in the Israelite Conception of God* (1942). For the view adopted above see F. F. Bruce, *Biblical Exegesis in the Qumran Texts* (1960), p. 65; H. L. Ellison, *The Centrality of the Messianic Idea for the Old Testament* (1953), pp. 13-15.
[19] J. T. Milik, 'Problèmes de la littérature hénochique à la lumière des fragments araméens de Qumran', *HTR* 64, 1971, pp. 333-378.
[20] C. Colpe, *TDNT* VIII, pp. 406-430. Colpe's article includes an extensive critique of other suggested derivations.
[21] F. H. Borsch, *The Son of Man in Myth and History* (1967).
[22] M. D. Hooker, *The Son of Man in Mark* (1967), pp. 11-74.
[23] N. Perrin, *Rediscovering the Teaching of Jesus* (1967), pp. 164-173.
[24] R. Leivestad, 'Exit the Apocalyptic Son of Man', *NTS* 18, 1971-72, pp. 243-267; a fuller version of the argument is to be found in 'Der apokalyptische Menschensohn ein theologisches Phantom', *Annual of the Swedish Theological Institute* 6, 1968, pp. 49-105.
[25] P. Vielhauer, *Aufsätze zum Neuen Testament* (1965), pp. 55-91, 92-140; N. Perrin, *Rediscovering the Teaching of Jesus* (1967), pp. 173-199; *A Modern Pilgrimage* (1974), pp. 57-83; H. Conzelmann, *An Outline of the Theology of the New Testament* (1969), pp. 131-137.
[26] C. Cullmann, *The Christology of the New Testament* (1959), pp. 137-192; V. Taylor, *The Names of Jesus* (1953), pp. 25-35; R. Maddox, 'The Function of the Son of Man according to the Synoptic Gospels', *NTS* 15, 1968-69. pp. 45-74; F. F. Bruce, *This is That* (1968), pp. 26-30, 96-99; M. D. Hooker, *The Son of Man in Mark* (1967); F. H. Borsch, *The Son of Man in Myth and History* (1967).

[27] M. D. Hooker, *op. cit.*, pp. 27-30; *cf.* C. F. D. Moule, *The Phenomenon of the New Testament* (1967), pp. 82-99 (a reprint of his article, 'From Defendant to Judge — and Deliverer', originally published in *SNTSB* III, 1952, pp. 40-53); C. K. Barrett, 'The Background of Mark 10:45', in A. J. B. Higgins (ed.), *New Testament Essays* (1959), pp. 1-18. Against this view see especially R. T. France, *Jesus and the Old Testament* (1971), pp. 128-130.

[28] R. Bultmann, *The History of the Synoptic Tradition*[2] (1968), p. 152; *Theology of the New Testament* (1952), I, pp. 28-32; G. Bornkamm, *Jesus of Nazareth* (1960), pp. 228-231.

[29] H. E. Tödt, *The Son of Man in the Synoptic Tradition* (1965).

[30] F. Hahn, *The Titles of Jesus in Christology* (1969), ch. 1; R. H. Fuller, *The Foundations of New Testament Christology* (1965), pp. 119-125, 143-155.

[31] A. J. B. Higgins, *Jesus and the Son of Man* (1964).

[32] C. Colpe, *TDNT* VIII, pp. 430-461.

[33] E. Schweizer, 'Der Menschensohn', *ZNW* 50, 1959, pp. 185-209; 'The Son of Man', *JBL* 79, 1960, pp. 119-129 (the quotation is from pp. 121f.); 'The Son of Man Again', *NTS* 9, 1962-63, pp. 256-261 (the first and third of these articles are reprinted in E. Schweizer, *Neotestamentica* (1963), pp. 56-84, 85-92); *The Good News according to Mark* (1971), pp. 166-171. *Cf.* W. Stott, ' "Son of Man — a title of Abasement', *Exp.T* 83, 1971-72, pp. 278-281.

[34] R. Leivestad, 'Exit the Apocalyptic Son of Man', *NTS* 18, 1971-72, p. 262.

[35] G. Vermes, *Jesus the Jew* (1973), p. 186. For a similar view see J. C. O'Neill, 'The Silence of Jesus', *NTS* 15, 1968-69, pp. 153-167, especially pp. 158-162.

[36] Jn. 9:35 looks like an exception to this rule, but here the use of the title 'Son of man' may be due to the theological requirements of the situation.

[37] P. Vielhauer, *Aufsätze zum Neuen Testament* (1965), pp. 55-91.

[38] Vielhauer is right in his claim that no saying of Jesus associates the Son of man with the kingdom of God, but wrong in the conclusion he draws from it; see J. Jeremias, *New Testament Theology* (1971), I, pp. 267f.

[39] See above, p. 51.

[40] J. Jeremias, *op. cit.*, pp. 262-264.

[41] See my article in *NTS* 12, 1965-66, especially pp. 339ff.

[42] J. Jeremias, *op. cit.*, pp. 275f.

[43] *Cf.* H. E. Tödt, *The Son of Man in the Synoptic Tradition* (1965); R. Maddox, 'The Function of the Son of Man according to the Synoptic Gospels', *NTS* 15, 1968-69, pp. 45-74.

[44] R. T. France, *Jesus and the Old Testament* (1971), pp. 110-135.

[45] R. T. France, *op. cit.*

[46] J. Jeremias, *op. cit.*, pp. 264f.

[47] The Johannine material itself constitutes a vast area for study which has had to be passed over in silence here. Recent work includes: S. S. Smalley, 'The Johannine Son of Man Sayings', *NTS* 15, 1968-69, pp. 278-301; B. Lindars, 'The Son of Man in the Johannine Christology', in B. Lindars and S. S. Smalley (eds.), *Christ and Spirit in the New*

*Testament* (1973), pp. 43-60; R. Maddox, 'The Function of the Son of Man in the Gospel of John', in R. Banks (ed.), *Reconciliation and Hope* (1974), pp. 186-204.

[48] Obvious examples include Mt. 16:13 (*cf.* Mk. 8:27) and Mt. 5:11 (contrast Lk. 6:22).

[49] The two areas where 'Son of man' is under suspicion of being added to the tradition are *a*. the prophecies of the passion and resurrection, and *b*. the prophecies of the future coming and glory of the Son of man. If our thesis is correct, however, the early church will have done no more than give fuller precision and colour to what Jesus himself had already said.

[50] The most recent discussions include C. F. D. Moule, 'Neglected Features in the Problem of "the Son of Man"', in J. Gnilka (ed.), *Neues Testament und Kirche* (1974), pp. 413-428; B. Lindars, 'Re-enter the Apocalyptic Son of Man', *NTS* 22, 1975-76, pp. 52-72; R. Pesch and R. Schnackenburg (eds.), *Jesus und der Menschensohn* (1975).

# 5 ARE YOU THE CHRIST?

We began our investigation of the titles of Jesus from the fairly firm evidence that he spoke of himself as the Son of man, a phrase that was used almost exclusively by himself and was not part of the church's vocabulary to any significant extent. The other titles, which we now proceed to investigate, are ones which appear rarely, if at all, on the lips of Jesus but were the common stock-in-trade of the early church, and the essential problem which confronts us is how these titles came to be applied to Jesus and what historical basis there was for applying them to him. There is perhaps not so wide a cleavage of opinions over these titles as there is regarding 'Son of man', but nevertheless scholarly opinion is still in a state of flux regarding them. In the case of the title 'Messiah' we have an up-to-date survey available in the final volume of Kittel's *Theological Dictionary of the New Testament*, and this sets out the basic background material especially well.[1]

### The Jewish use of the title

With the term 'Christ' we are firmly established in Jewish soil. The Greek word *Christos*, derived from the verb *chriō*, 'to smear, anoint', is an adjective which usually means 'anointed', *i.e.* rubbed or smeared with oil. It is used in biblical Greek as a translation of the Hebrew noun *mashiach*, 'anointed one'; the word *Messias* is a Greek transliteration which was largely supplanted by the native Greek word.[2] Although in New Testament times 'Christ' developed into a name for Jesus (*e.g.* Rom. 5:6, 8; 1 Cor. 1:12, 17; Heb. 3:6; 9:11), the word is basically a description or title of a person with a particular function.

In the Old Testament three types of people were appointed to their offices by a ceremony involving anointing: kings, priests and prophets. The king especially was referred to as 'the anointed of Yahweh', and there are several accounts of the anointing of rulers. The language suggests that it is really Yahweh who appoints and anoints the king, and in so doing grants him authority and glory. In the same way the high priest and also the other priests were appointed to office by anointing. The evidence for the anointing of prophets, however, is scanty (1 Ki. 19:16; Ps. 105:15; Sirach 48:8), and it is not clear whether there was a literal counterpart to the way in which the prophet claims to have been anointed by Yahweh and to have received his Spirit in Isaiah 61:1.

The term 'anointed' is not used in the Old Testament with reference to a future king descended from David. The significance of Daniel 9:25 is not clear;[3] Zechariah 4:14 speaks of two anointed ones who appear to be Joshua the high priest and Zerubbabel the ruler. But if the actual term is not used, there is a clear hope that one day God will raise up a king, descended from David and like David in character, to rule over Israel in peace and righteousness.

This hope continued into New Testament times, but it must be emphasized that the actual term 'Messiah' or 'anointed one' is comparatively rare (though not as rare as 'Son of man').[4] The hope of a coming king is found in the Psalms of Solomon 17:36; 18:6, 8; and this figure takes on an apocalyptic colouring in 4 Ezra 7:27f.; 12:31f. and other apocalyptic writings. Of particular interest is the expectation in the Qumran scrolls of two anointed figures side by side, as in Zechariah 4:14, one a high priest descended from Levi and the other a king descended from Judah (1QS 9:11; 4QTest; but CD 12:23 refers to the Messiah of Aaron and Israel). The high priest takes precedence over the king. It is interesting that in one of the texts Isaiah 61:1f. is taken up and applied to a prophet who functions at the end-time.[5] Finally, various Jewish prayers which may contain elements going back to New Testament times express the hope of the coming of an anointed one descended from

David, and when Simon bar Koseba led the Jews in their
second war of independence against Rome (AD 132-135) he
was hailed by a leading rabbi as 'the king, the Messiah'.[6]
This brief survey of the evidence has been confined to the
actual use of the phrase 'anointed one'. But it would be
wrong to think that the Messianic hope is to be found only
where the actual word is used. Jewish expectation was considerably fuller and took a variety of forms; there was plenty
of scope for imaginative concepts of what God would do in
the future. Recently K. Berger has argued that we should not
think that the Jewish Messianic hope was expressed in thoroughly political-nationalistic terms; he claims that the hope
of 'David's son' was modelled on the historical figure of
Solomon as a wise man possessed of divine knowledge and
able to overcome demonic forces arrayed in opposition to
truth.[7] But this can only have been one strand among many
in Jewish thought; it may, however, be the one that influenced
the development of the Christian idea of the Messiah. This is
manifestly an area for research.

## Did Jesus use the title?

At least one thing is clear about the title of Messiah in the
Gospels: it occurs comparatively rarely. In the Synoptic
Gospels there are no more than six possible cases of its use by
Jesus before his death, and two of these are clearly editorial
clarifications by Matthew of the corresponding sayings in
Mark (Mt. 16:20; cf. Mk. 8:29f. Mt. 24:5; cf. 24:23; Mk.
13:6). On one occasion Jesus warns against people who will
falsely claim that the Christ has appeared (Mk. 13:21), and
once he poses the question as to how the Christ can be the
son of David (Mk. 12:35). In neither case is Jesus clearly
identifying himself to his hearers as the Messiah. This leaves
only the sayings where Jesus promises reward to anyone who
gives a cup of water to the disciples 'because you bear the
name of Christ' (Mk. 9:41) and tells the disciples that they
'have one master, the Christ' (Mt. 23:10). It is not surprising
that with such weak evidence available it has been denied
that Jesus used the title with regard to himself, and it is not
difficult for scholars who take this line to regard the couple

of sayings that suggest otherwise as modifications or creations by the early church.[8]

This, of course, is not the whole story. There are two areas where other people speak of Jesus as the Christ, and the Gospels show that there was some interest in the term among the populace. The first of these areas is the account of the trial and crucifixion of Jesus. There is little room for doubt that Jesus was put to death as one who was regarded as a pretender to Messiahship or kingship. This is the issue that emerges in the examination of Jesus before Pilate, and it was under the title of 'The King of the Jews' that he suffered crucifixion. The crucial question is whether Jesus himself accepted the charge. Although a number of writers have suggested that Jesus may have had sympathies with the Zealots and it has even been claimed that he was a Zealot,[9] the case that Jesus was really aiming at political revolution and the assumption of kingship belongs to the realm of fantasy.[10] Nevertheless, one is bound to ask why this particular charge was urged against him and whether there was any basis in his conduct for accusing him of claiming to be the Messiah. Why did the term 'Messiah' come into the picture, especially when we have no record of its use by revolutionary leaders in the first century?

This leads us to the difficult problem of the Jewish trial of Jesus at which the high priest is reported to have asked Jesus, 'Are you the Christ?' and Jesus replied, 'I am' (Mk. 14:61f.). Essentially there are three interpretations of this dialogue. First, there is the view that the account of the trial is to greater or less extent fictitious, so that no reliable evidence can be drawn from it.[11] Second, there is the view that, if the dialogue is based on history, Jesus' reply should be understood as a denial of Messiahship; this view depends upon the theory that the form of reply found in Matthew 26:64 and Luke 22:67-70 is original ('You say (that I am)') and that it is tantamount to a denial.[12] Third, there is the view that Jesus' reply (as in the second interpretation) is equivocal and can be regarded as a qualified affirmative, 'Yes, but that is your way of putting it, not mine.'[13] Linguistically this last possibility is well-supported.

The other narrative of the same kind is the account of the

dialogue at Caesarea Philippi in which Jesus asked the disciples their opinion as to who he was and Peter replied 'You are the Christ' (Mk. 8:29). Thereupon Jesus told them not to tell anybody. As it stands, the narrative implies that Jesus tacitly accepted the description, and the nature of the Gospel story up to that point appears to be designed to provide the evidence on which such an assessment of Jesus could rightly be based. However, the historicity of the narrative has been challenged. The simplest argument is that Peter's confession is a statement of the early church's belief in Jesus read back into the period of his earthly life. A more sophisticated approach is to argue that Mark 8:30 and 31-32a are later additions to the narrative, the former being a piece of Marcan theology (the 'Messianic secret' motif) and the latter a separate and late 'Son of man' saying; subtraction of these two elements and the linking clauses means that Jesus' rebuke to Peter, 'Get behind me, Satan!' was originally his repudiation of Peter's confession as something of diabolical inspiration. Jesus on this view flatly rejected Messiahship.[14] This rewriting of the incident is improbable, to say the least. Even, however, as the story stands, Jesus interprets Messiahship in terms of the suffering of the Son of man, and strongly repudiates any other understanding of it; it is impossible to resist the impression that what Peter meant by Messiahship was not the same as the role that Jesus felt called to play.

Such is the evidence in the Gospels for the use of the actual title by Jesus. What do scholars make of it? The first, and apparently the easiest, solution is the theory that Jesus did not claim to be Messiah because he did not work in terms of this idea. He did not use the title himself, and he did not accept it when others applied it to him.[15] On this view the title was applied to him by the early church after the resurrection—the way in which this happened being discussed in the next section. The impetus towards applying it to him came from the fact of his crucifixion as a Messianic pretender.

It was in connection with this view that W. Wrede developed his famous hypothesis of the 'Messianic secret'. This theory has undergone many modifications, but basically it was an attempt to deal with the fact that in Mark the Messiahship of

Jesus is largely kept secret from the people. Wrede postulated that it was only after the resurrection that Jesus was regarded as the Messiah, and at first his earthly ministry was not regarded as Messianic in character. Consequently, there was no evidence for his Messiahship in the earliest Gospel material. At a later stage the church claimed that Jesus did know that he was the Messiah during his earthly life, and it explained the lack of evidence for this by saying that Jesus did not reveal his Messiahship openly but deliberately kept it secret, except from his disciples. As a result Mark's portrayal of the ministry is said to be full of historical improbabilities.[16]

In this form the theory is palpably weak; it directs attention to some difficult phenomena in the Gospels, but fails to offer a convincing explanation of them. But the most important objection to it is that there is no evidence that the story of Jesus ever existed in a non-Messianic form. The earliest ascertainable forms of the traditions about Jesus are 'Messianic' in the broad sense.[17] And, so far as Wrede's statement of the theory is concerned, this is crucial. For, although it is a theory of a 'Messianic' secret, the actual term 'Messiah' scarcely figures in the formulation of the secret (except in Mk.8:29f.). [18]

Consequently, the tendency among recent scholars has been to invert the theory: the original tradition about Jesus was heavily 'Messianic', in the sense that it depicted Jesus as a powerful wonder-worker and a figure of glory, but the later church (especially in the person of Mark) attempted to correct this picture in the light of the apostolic preaching of the cross by emphasizing that Jesus is the Messiah only insofar as he suffered, was rejected and died on the cross. Jesus cannot be known as the Messiah before it has become clear that he is a crucified Messiah, and he cannot be known as such except by those who are prepared to suffer self-denial and tread the path of humble discipleship.[19]

There can be no doubt that this kind of statement of the theory does fuller justice to the evidence which it seeks to explain. The important point in the present context is the admission that the earliest Gospel tradition has a broadly 'Messianic' character. Jesus performed Messianic acts, such as the entry to Jerusalem and the cleansing of the Temple. Here we must recall the results of our earlier discussion which suggested that this tradition reflected Jesus' own consciousness of his role. In other words, the evidence is against the view that Jesus did not claim to be Messiah *because* he was not conscious of undertaking some kind of Messianic role.

But the fact that Jesus was conscious of some such role does not necessarily lead to the conclusion that he accepted the title of 'Messiah'. We must now, therefore, look at other assessments of the evidence regarding the use of the title. A second possibility is that Jesus did not accept the title because he regarded himself only as 'Messiah-designate'. This view is attributed to Bultmann and his followers by R. N. Longenecker, but so far as I can tell this is a misrepresentation of their views; it was, however, held by some earlier scholars.[20]

A third view is that Jesus rejected the current Jewish ideal of Messiahship but held to some private ideal of his own. This view is widely held among scholars of a conservative persuasion. It is advocated, for example, by O. Cullmann, who argues that the Jewish ideal was intensely nationalistic and therefore rejected by Jesus. Along with the false ideal it was necessary to reject the misleading title. This would give a historical basis for the 'Messianic secret': Jesus would not allow himself to be known by a misleading title. The case for understanding the 'Messianic secret' in this way has been strongly advocated by J. D. G. Dunn.[21] It may well be that Jesus' choice of 'Son of man' as a self-designation is to be linked with his avoidance of 'Messiah': the former term was not so open to misrepresentation as the latter.

A fourth type of theory is that suggested by D. Flusser, J. C. O'Neill and R. N. Longenecker, who suggest that there was a belief that no-one could claim to be the Messiah until he had accomplished the work of the Messiah.[22] This pattern of action is to be traced in the Qumran Teacher of Righteousness and Simon bar Koseba, both of whom were conscious of a divine calling but did not validate it by the use of titles. Jesus could not claim the title until he had given proof that he had done the work of the Messiah. He was publicly declared to be Messiah 'not just *after* his passion and resurrection but *because* of his passion and resurrection'.[23] By itself this is probably

not a sufficient explanation of Jesus' attitude, but it sup-
plements the previous view.

By combining the third and fourth views in this way we
obtain a picture that does justice to the fact that Jesus' activity aroused Messianic speculations, although he himself was
decidedly reticent in confirming such speculations. The
decisive factor is, then, not the actual use of the title, but the
evidence that Jesus understood his task in 'Messianic' terms in
the narrow sense. Evidence in support of this position was
cited earlier, but if our argument is sound Jesus was reinter-
preting the category of Messiahship, and therefore the citing
of evidence regarding activities that contemporary Judaism
saw as Messianic may seem irrelevant. Indeed, this may point
to an obvious objection to our case: if Jesus did not use the
title of 'Messiah', and if his views of 'Messiahship' were not
those of Judaism, what evidence is there that it was 'Messiahship' that he was interpreting? May not this whole category
be irrelevant to his way of thinking? May it not equally well
be the case that it was the early church which redefined
Messiahship in the light of Jesus' actual ministry and thus
made use of a new connotation which had not been used by
Jesus?[24]

Three points may be made in reply to this objection. The
first is that ideas about the Messiah were in the air, and it
would be most surprising if Jesus had not had to formulate
his own attitude to the question. As O. Cullmann points
out, 'The title expresses a continuity between the task he
had to fulfil and the Old Testament.'[25] It is, therefore, unlikely that Jesus would simply have rejected the idea — all the
more so if he operated with the term 'Son of man' which had
Messianic associations.[26] Second, it is most unlikely that the
term 'Christ' would have come to have so large a place in the
thought of the early church if there had not been some prep-
aration for it in the ministry of Jesus; the theory that the early
church applied the term to Jesus simply because it had been
falsely applied to him at his trial and because it contained
useful theological possibilities is highly improbable — especially if we may use an *argumentum ad hominem*, since at least
some of the advocates of this view seem highly doubtful

whether the resurrection, which is supposed to have triggered
off the process of Christological thinking, actually took
place. [27] Third, although Messianism was understood in a political fashion by many Jews, there is evidence that more spiritual
views of it did exist, and these were recognized by some
people in the ministry of Jesus. [28] These points make it
probable that the Gospels are right in suggesting that the
question of Messiahship did arise during the ministry of
Jesus and that Jesus himself sought to fulfil the Messianic
role in a new way.

### Jesus as Messiah in the early church
Both F. Hahn and R. H. Fuller claim that in the very earliest
days of the church the title 'Messiah' was not applied to Jesus.
For the first Palestinian Christians he was the 'Son of man'
who was expected to come on the clouds, rather than the living Lord exalted in heaven. The title of Messiah was also used
with regard to this future expectation of the coming of Jesus,
since already in Jewish apocalyptic there was a certain tendency to fuse the figures of the Son of man and the Messiah.
Various passages are cited as evidence of this belief: Mark
13:21f. (which warns against the future coming of false
Messiahs); Mark 14:61f. (where Messiah and Son of man are
identified); Matthew 25:31-46 (where the 'King' participates
in the final judgment); Revelation 11:15; 20:4, 6 (where the
future reign of the Messiah is proclaimed); and especially
Acts 3:20f. In this last passage J. A. T. Robinson recognized
that we may have the most primitive Christology of all. [29]
He argued that the text refers to the appointment of Jesus
as the Christ at the parousia, and that such a concept must
be more primitive than statements which identify the earthly
Jesus or the risen Jesus as the Messiah. [30]
    Hahn then argues that, when the early church began to
think of Jesus as the exalted one, it was natural to use the title
Messiah in this connection also, and he cites as evidence Mark
12:35-37 (regarded as a creation by the early church) and Acts
2:34-36; in both of these texts 'Lord' and 'Christ' are titles
of the risen and exalted Jesus. [31] It was only apparently at a
third stage (but still within the area of Palestinian Jewish

Christianity) that the title Messiah was linked to the suffering of Jesus; this was the result of his having been crucified under the name of 'the King of the Jews', and the evidence for this use of the title is found in its earliest form in 1 Corinthians 15:3-5 which is generally regarded as a Palestinian formula.[32] So the title which had originally been used of Jesus' future coming was now attached to his death, and then in the Hellenistic Jewish church the title began to be associated with the tradition of Jesus as a worker of miracles.

By the time that we reach the Hellenistic Gentile mission the title 'Christ' had begun to lose its significance and to be more of a name for Jesus.[33]

The key point in Hahn's reconstruction is his thesis that the earliest application of the title Christ was to the future activity of Jesus. But this is a most uncertain hypothesis, and the evidence is strongly against it. In the first place, we have to remember that the development from the 'future' use to the 'passion' use, which Hahn postulates, all took place within the Palestinian Jewish stage of Christianity. Now according to R. H. Fuller the 'passion' use had developed within two or three years of the crucifixion.[34] This period of time is far too short for us to be able to chart Christological development within it, and we have no historical framework into which the evidence can be slotted with any degree of certainty. We may well suspect that Hahn is trying to be impossibly precise.

Second, Hahn's case depends to some extent upon his thesis that the early church concentrated its initial attention on the future activity of Jesus and not upon his exaltation or his death. The evidence for this thesis is to be found in Hahn's treatment of the Son of man sayings (which we have already had reason to question) and especially upon his understanding of the use of 'Lord'; we shall examine this issue below.

Third, the texts cited by Hahn do not prove his case. The exegesis offered of Acts 3:20f. is faulty, and the text should be interpreted to mean that the One who has *already* been ordained as the Christ will return at the parousia; the stress is not on Jesus' ordination to be the Christ but on his ordination to be the Christ *for the Jews* to whom he was first sent

(Acts 3:26).[35] Jesus, therefore, is not the Messiah-designate, but the Messiah, a statement which fits in perfectly with Acts 2:36. As for the other texts cited, none of these can be shown to have arisen in the earliest Palestinian church before other Christological statements, although of course they do show that the Messiah was expected to act in the future. But if the texts cannot be shown to have been created at this particular stage, they cannot provide evidence for Hahn's particular theory.

Fourth, we can be reasonably certain that the title 'Christ' was associated with the death and resurrection of Jesus in the Palestinian church. In 1 Corinthians 15:3-5 Paul cites an early tradition, or combination of traditions, in which the term 'Christ' is the subject of credal-type statements referring to his death and resurrection. The Semitic background of the tradition is beyond doubt.[36] What is not absolutely clear is whether the term 'Christ' was the original form of the subject; it is arguable that originally such statements would be made about Jesus, and that the earliest statements would be of the form 'Jesus died and rose from the dead, and so he is the Christ', and that the present tradition already assumes the identification of Jesus as the Christ. This is a valid point, but it is not so certain that it supports the view, advocated by W. Kramer, that the title Christ was first introduced into this kind of statement by Greek-speaking Jewish Christianity.[37] In any case, there were Greek-speaking Christians in Jerusalem from the outset. The point, therefore, is not beyond doubt, but it is most reasonable to suppose that the title of Christ was associated with the death and resurrection of Jesus from an early date.

In Acts 2:36 we are indeed given the kind of argument that was doubtless used. Jesus was raised from the dead by God: 'Let all the house of Israel therefore know assuredly that God has made him both Lord and Christ, this Jesus whom you crucified.' If we ask why it was that the early Christians applied this particular title to Jesus in the light of his resurrection, the most reasonable explanation would appear to lie in a combination of the facts that Jesus' claims to be a 'Messianic' figure of some kind had now been vindicated by God and that the title of 'Messiah' was readily suggested for use by the *titulus* 'The King of the Jews' affixed to the cross. At the same time we should perhaps not be too hasty in dismissing the evidence that the risen Jesus instructed his disciples in the fact that the Messiah must suffer (Lk. 24:26f., 46). The use of the title 'king' was politically dangerous and misleading (Acts 17:7); the term 'Messiah' had other associations, was perhaps not in common use to any great extent,[38] and in its Greek form as 'Christ' it quickly lost its specific content and became merely a name for Jesus.

In this way the title of Messiah or Christ was probably applied to Jesus as a result of the resurrection. In the early church it was especially associated with statements regarding his death and resurrection, as a series of formulae isolated by W. Kramer clearly indicates.[39] Under the influence of the actual ministry of Jesus the content of Messiahship was increasingly understood in new ways. The elements of rule were subordinated to those of deliverance and salvation. The Old Testament was explored for indications of the character and career of the Messiah, and motifs attached to other titles were applied to it. There is a whole area here for detailed study and exposition, but this task must lie outside our present scope.

# NOTES

[1] W. Grundmann, F. Hesse, M. de Jonge and A. S. van der Woude, *TDNT* IX, pp. 493-580. See also O. Cullmann, *The Christology of the New Testament* (1959), pp. 111-136; F. Hahn, *The Titles of Jesus in Christology* (1969), pp. 136-239; R. H. Fuller, *The Foundations of New Testament Christology* (1965), pp. 23-31, 63f., 109-111, 158-162, 184-186, 191f., 230; W. Kramer, *Christ, Lord, Son of God* (1966), pp. 19-64, 133-150; G. Vermes, *Jesus the Jew* (1973), pp. 129-159.
[2] *Messias* is derived from the Aramaic form *meshicha*. It is found in the New Testament only in Jn. 1:41; 4:25.
[3] Although the verse has been traditionally interpreted as a prophecy of the Messiah, it is not so identified in the New Testament.
[4] M. de Jonge, 'The Word "Anointed" in the Time of Jesus', *Nov.T* 8, 1966, pp. 132-148; J. C. O'Neill, *The Theology of Acts in its Historical Setting* (1961), pp. 121-123 (not in the second edition, 1970).
[5] 11Q Melchizedek. *Cf.* M. de Jonge and A. S. van der Woude, '11Q Melchizedek and the New Testament', *NTS* 12, 1965-66, pp. 301-326.

[6] A. S. van der Woude, *TDNT* IX, pp. 521-523.

[7] K. Berger, 'Die königlichen Messiastraditionen des Neuen Testaments', *NTS* 20, 1973-74, pp. 1-44; 'Zum Problem der Messianität Jesu', *ZTK* 71, 1974, pp. 1-30.

[8] The evidence in John does not basically alter the picture. Only in Jn. 17:3 is the use of the title apparently attributed to Jesus himself, but this is probably a comment by the Evangelist (B. F. Westcott, *St. John* (1822), p. 240). Jesus is acknowledged as Messiah in Jn. 1:41;4: 25f., 29.

[9] This view has been attributed to S. G. F. Brandon (see his book, *Jesus and the Zealots* (1967), and the comment by G. Vermes, *Jesus the Jew* (1973), p. 49), but he has insisted that this is an incorrect assessment of his position (' "Jesus and the Zealots": A Correction', *NTS* 17, 1970-71, p. 453).

[10] M. Hengel, *Was Jesus a Revolutionist?* (1971) and *Victory over Violence* (1974).

[11] F. Hahn, *The Titles of Jesus in Christology* (1969), pp. 159f.; E. Lohse, *TDNT* VII, pp. 867-870; *cf.* P. Winter, *On the Trial of Jesus* (1961). On the other side see J. Blinzler, *The Trial of Jesus* (1959); D. R. Catchpole, 'The Problem of the Historicity of the Sanhedrin Trial', in E. Bammel (ed.), *The Trial of Jesus* (1970), pp. 47-65.

[12] O. Cullmann, *The Christology of the New Testament* (1959), pp. 118-121. Cullmann, however, virtually admits that Jesus' answer is equivocal.

[13] D. R. Catchpole, 'The Answer of Jesus to Caiaphas (Matt. xxvi. 64)', *NTS* 17, 1970-71, pp. 213-226.

[14] F. Hahn, *op. cit.*, pp. 223-228; R. H. Fuller, *The Foundations of New Testament Christology* (1965), p. 109. The suggestion is rejected by W. G. Kümmel, *The Theology of the New Testament* (1974), pp. 69f., for the excellent reason that the early church would not have handed down an account in which Jesus rejected Peter's confession as Satanic.

[15] G. Vermes, *Jesus the Jew* (1973), p. 149.

[16] W. Wrede, *The Messianic Secret* (1971) (belated English translation of *Das Messiasgeheimnis in den Evangelien*, 1901, reprinted 1963). For surveys of subsequent modifications of the theory see B. G. Powley, 'The Purpose of the Messianic Secret: A Brief Survey', *Exp.T* 80, 1968-69, pp. 308-310; D. E. Aune, 'The Problem of the Messianic Secret', *Nov.T* 11, 1969, pp. 1-31; J. D. G. Dunn, 'The Messianic Secret in Mark', *Tyn.B* 21, 1970, pp. 92-117.

[17] See chapter 3.

[18] It has been suggested that 'Son of God secret' would be a more apt title.

[19] E. Schweizer, *The Good News according to Mark* (1971), pp. 54-56. *Cf.* the survey of recent theories in R. P. Martin, *Mark: Evangelist and Theologian* (1972), pp. 140-162.

[20] R. N. Longenecker, 'The Messianic Secret in the Light of Recent Discoveries', *EQ* 41, 1969, pp. 207-215, especially pp. 209f. (This article is substantially incorporated in *The Christology of Early Jewish Christianity* (1970), pp. 66-80.) See G. Dalman, *The Words of Jesus* (1909), pp. 315f.

[21] O. Cullmann, *The Christology of the New Testament* (1959), pp. 126f.; J. D. G. Dunn, *art. cit.*

[22] D. Flusser, 'Two Notes on the Midrash on 2 Sam. vii', *Israel Exploration Journal* 9, 1959, pp. 99-109, especially 107-109'; R. N. Longenecker, *art. cit.*; J. C. O'Neill, 'The Silence of Jesus', *NTS* 15, 1968-69, pp. 153-167.

[23] R. N. Longenecker, *art. cit.*, p. 215.

[24] This is essentially the position of F. Hahn.

[25] O. Cullmann, *op. cit.*, p. 126.

[26] See above, pp. 66f., for the view that from the beginning the figure in Dn. 7:13 was regarded as 'Messianic'. A strict dichotomy between 'Messiah' and 'Son of man' is unjustified.

[27] This point could certainly be pressed against R. Bultmann.

[28] K. Berger, 'Die königlichen Messiastraditionen des Neuen Testaments', *NTS* 20, 1973-74, pp. 1-44. Perhaps more importance should be attached to the view that the Messiah was regarded as a figure endowed with the Spirit; *cf.* W. C. van Unnik, 'Jesus the Christ', *NTS* 8, 1961-62, pp. 101-116.

[29] J. A. T. Robinson, 'The Most Primitive Christology of All?', *JTS* n.s. 7, 1956, pp. 177-189, reprinted in *Twelve New Testament Studies* (1962), pp. 139-153.

[30] R. H. Fuller (*The Foundations of New Testament Christology* (1965), pp. 158f.) questions whether this is the most primitive Christology of all, but states that it is at least more primitive than the concept in Acts 2:36.

[31] F. Hahn, *The Titles of Jesus in Christology* (1969), pp. 168-172.

[32] The basic study is J. Jeremias, *The Eucharistic Words of Jesus* (1966), pp. 101-103. The case has been questioned by H. Conzelmann, *An Outline of the Theology of the New Testament* (1969), pp. 65f., but even he allows that the passage is ultimately based on Jerusalem tradition.

[33] R. H. Fuller, *op. cit.*, p. 230.

[34] *Ibid.*, p. 161.

[35] F. F. Bruce, 'The Speeches in Acts—Thirty Years After', in R. J. Banks (ed.), *Reconciliation and Hope* (1974), pp. 53-68, especially pp. 67f.

[36] See n. 32, above. Also B. Klappert, 'Zur Frage des semitischen oder griechischen Urtextes von 1 Kor. xv. 3-5', *NTS* 13, 1966-67, pp. 168-173.

[37] W. Kramer, *Christ, Lord, Son of God* (1966), pp. 38-44.

[38] See n. 4, above.

[39] W. Kramer (*op. cit.*, pp. 20-32) cites Rom. 5:6, 8; 1 Pet. 3:18; Rom. 6:3-9; 8:34; 14:9.

# 6 JESUS IS LORD

The mark of a Christian in the early church was that he was prepared to confess his faith in the words 'Jesus (Christ) is Lord' (Rom. 10:9; 1 Cor. 12:3; Phil. 2:11). There were, as Paul remarks, many 'gods' and many 'lords' adored by men in the first century, but for the Christian 'there is one God, the Father, . . . and one Lord, Jesus Christ' (1 Cor. 8:6). From an early date Jesus was being spoken of as Lord, as is evidenced by the survival of the Aramaic formula 'Maranatha' in the Greek-speaking church (1 Cor. 16:22). But what was the significance of this title, what did it mean when it was applied to Jesus, and how did its use develop? [1]

## The meaning of the word 'Lord'

The word 'lord' (Greek, *kyrios*) was one of the most common terms in New Testament times, and designated a person possessing power and authority. It was used basically to denote the owner of property and slaves, one who has the right to do as he wishes with his own property.[2] By a natural extension of language the word was used of any person occupying a position of superiority, and in particular the vocative form was used as a form of address by slaves to their masters, and in general as a courteous and respectful form of address.

Of particular importance was the use of 'lord' to designate pagan deities, and the corresponding use of the word 'slave' to designate the worshipper. But this usage arose mostly in Egypt, Syria and Asia Minor, and represents a Greek translation of an indigenous title.[3] In the same areas of the world rulers were also addressed by this title. During the first century the title was used for the Roman emperor, but there is some dispute whether this title merely indicated the supreme power of the emperor or also attributed to him some sort of divine position. Certainly Domitian liked to be called *'Dominus et deus noster'* (Our Lord and God), and in the eastern part of the Roman Empire there was a strong tendency to regard the emperor as a god. On the whole it is probable that the boundary between humanity and divinity was blurred, so that the emperor could easily be thought of as more than human. If the emperor became a god when he died — Vespasian, when dying, said with a touch of sarcastic humour, 'I think that I am becoming a god' — it was not difficult to think that a man destined to become a god was already in some sense divine.[4]

### The Jewish usage

In the Hebrew Old Testament God is frequently called 'Yahweh'. It is well known that the Jews came to regard this name as so sacred that they felt it wrong to utter it. Accordingly, when they came to the word in their Scriptures they did not say it and substituted the word *Adonai,* which means '(my) Lord'. When the Hebrew text, which was originally composed only of consonants, had vowel marks added to it, the sacred name 'YHWH' was written with the vowels of *'Adonai'* as a sign to the reader to pronounce the latter word instead. Now in the Greek translation of the Old Testament, the Septuagint, we find that the name of God is regularly represented by the word 'Lord' (*kyrios*). The problem is that of the relationship between the Jewish and the Greek use: which gave rise to the other? The 'obvious' answer is that the Greek usage is modelled on the Jewish (Hebrew) custom, but it has been argued that the influence was in the opposite direction. The problem has been complicated by the uncertainty regarding the original practice of the Greek translators of the Old Testament. The earliest fragments of Greek translations show that *kyrios* was not used, but that some representation of the letters of 'YHWH' was used. These complications have been underlined by P. Vielhauer, [5] but it should be noted that the use of *kyrios* is found in Septuagint manuscripts from the second century

AD, that the New Testament writers use *kyrios* in quoting
from the Old Testament, and that no convincing explanation
of this usage other than Jewish precedent has been given. It is,
therefore, most probable that *kyrios* was used with reference
to God by Greek-speaking Jews in New Testament times; it
was used as a translation of *adon*, 'lord', and as the equivalent
of 'Yahweh'.

Another difficult problem is the use of similar terms in
Aramaic. The Aramaic term for 'lord' is *mare*. This word was
used as a form of address (in the form *mari*, 'my lord'), and as
such it could be used both of God and of men. The difficulty
has been to know whether the word could be used absolutely
as a title ('the Lord') to refer to God. Older books argued that
this was not possible; the word was always used with some
kind of qualifier (*e.g.* 'the Lord of heaven and earth').[6] Recent
discoveries in the Qumran texts have shown that the absolute
form is used with reference to God.[7] Consequently, statements to the effect that Aramaic-speaking Jews would not
have used the Aramaic word *mare* to refer to God [8] are erroneous. Indeed the analogy of the Hebrew use of *adon* would
facilitate this usage.

### Jesus as Lord
We can begin our examination of the use of 'lord' in the New
Testament by noting that it is used in a number of places as a
title for God. This is what we would expect if the title was
already used in this way in the Septuagint. The striking thing
is that this use of the term is comparatively infrequent; W.
Foerster rightly comments that its use arises from its basic
attestation in the Bible, *i.e.* it is used in quotations from the
Old Testament and in passages which are heavily influenced
by the thought and style of the Old Testament.[9] This fact
indicates how much 'the Lord' came to be set aside as a
title for Jesus.

But how did this process begin? When we direct our attention
to the Gospels, we observe that the sayings where Jesus may
be referring to himself as 'the Lord' are very few indeed. In
Mark 11:3 the disciples are instructed to tell the people in
charge of the colt: 'The Lord has need of it', but this may

simply be a way of referring to Jesus' authority as a teacher (*cf.* Mk. 14:14).[10] More important for future developments is Mark 12: 35-37, in which Jesus cites Psalm 110:1 to show that the Messiah must be David's Lord (and *a fortiori* everybody else's Lord); but here no self-identification is openly made, although anybody who was beginning to wonder whether Jesus was the Messiah might make the appropriate application. But this is all,[11] and Mark and Matthew follow Jesus' example by not referring to him as 'the Lord' in their narratives. Luke, however, does do this, and thus demonstrates that the One who was known as Lord from his resurrection onwards was also in fact the Lord during his earthly ministry, demonstrating his authority in teaching and performing mighty works.

Alongside this 'narrative' use of 'Lord' we must set the use of the vocative form (*kyrie*) as an address to Jesus. This is found only once in Mark (7:28), but is very common in the other Gospels, and occurs alongside the vocatives '*rabbi*' and 'teacher'. *Kyrie* may represent the Aramaic forms *rabbi* or *mari*, but it is probable that the latter lies behind it.

P. Vielhauer makes the attempt to show that the use of *kyrie* in the Gospels does not reflect what actually happened during Jesus' lifetime (except perhaps in Mk. 7:28 and Lk. 7:6, both times on the lips of non-Jews); it has been introduced into the narrative by the Evangelists or by Hellenistic transmitters of the Gospel tradition.[12] But Luke regarded *kyrie* as equivalent to *rabbi* and in general the address does not seem to have had the connotation of divinity. It is improbable that we can reject all the uses in the Gospels as easily as Vielhauer suggests.

F. Hahn makes a case that Jesus was addressed as *mari*, a form of address that was suggestive of authority but not of divinity. He finds that it was very similar in meaning to *rabbi*, but that the Evangelists (especially Matthew) have a tendency to see more in it.[13] A different picture is given by G. Vermes, who argues that *kyrie* is used principally in miracle stories in Mark and Matthew but as a way of referring to a teacher in Luke. He claims that this fits in with Palestinian usage, and that it is highly probable that the picture in the Gospels is basically historical.[14] Vermes's evidence is on occasion strained, [15] but the essence of his case is sound. That 'Lord' was an appropriate title for a teacher seems certain (*cf.* Jn 13: 13f.; Lk. 6:46). This last passage is especially significant, for it shows that Jesus was recognized as a teacher who gave commands that were meant to be obeyed and not simply instruction or advice.[16]

## Jesus as the coming Lord

If we are looking for the earliest use of the title 'Lord' for Jesus in the primitive church, it is proper to begin with the clearly attested use of the Aramaic form *mare* found in the formula *maranatha*, cited by Paul in 1 Corinthians 16:22. This formula can mean 'our Lord, come' or 'our Lord has come' (or, with a *perfectum futuri*, virtually equivalent to a prophetic perfect, 'our Lord will come'), depending on how the original Aramaic is reconstructed.[17] Scholars no longer doubt that this formula goes back to the Palestinian Aramaic-speaking church; the theory of W. Bousset and R. Bultmann that it developed in a bi-lingual church (Damascus or Antioch) can no longer claim serious support.[18] What, then, did this formula mean in the Palestinian church? The evidence from what are probably Greek equivalents to the formula shows that it could have been understood in either of the two ways mentioned above, as an imperative ('Come, Lord Jesus!', Rev. 22:20), or as an indicative ('The Lord is at hand', Phil. 4:5). Support for the latter view has been produced by M. Black, who points out that the recently discovered fragments of Enoch found at Qumran (4Q Enoch) give us the Aramaic form of the passage cited in Jude 14f. (1 Enoch 1:9, 'Behold, the Lord came . . .'); although the words in question are missing from the fragmentary text, Black argues that the form of the quotation in Jude reflects an original Aramaic [*Ha'*] *Mara(n) 'atha'*, which would be equivalent to the formula in Paul.[19] This evidence, weak as it is, would give some confirmation to the view that what was at first a promise of the coming of the Lord could be turned into a prayer (compare Rev. 22:20a and b).

It has been argued that the Lord who was awaited was originally God rather than Jesus,[20] and this view might also be supported from the use of 1 Enoch 1:9 in Jude 14f., since the Enoch passage would originally have referred to God. But it is difficult, if not impossible, to visualize a situation in which the early Christians would have awaited the coming of God, especially if their hopes for the future were pinned on the coming of the Son of man, and it is much more probable that from the beginning the *maranatha* formula referred to Jesus. This is all the more likely since the formula appears to have been associated with the Lord's Supper (Didache 10:6).

But was this the earliest use of the title 'Lord' for Jesus? F. Hahn, as we have seen, is the leading advocate of this view. He points to various Synoptic texts which indicate the use of *kyrios* in relation to the last judgment (Mt. 7:21, 22; 25:11, 37, 44), and concludes that the early church used the title 'to express the exalted rank and authority of the One who was to return'.[21] Psalm 110:1 was originally understood to refer to the assumption of dignity by Jesus at the parousia; only as the parousia was delayed did the Hellenistic Jewish church begin to claim that Jesus had been exalted as Lord at the resurrection.

The weakness of this view is the same as in Hahn's reconstruction of the earliest use of 'Christ': the evidence that these texts were the earliest fruit of the church's Christological thinking is simply not there. But more important is the question whether it is likely that the early church first applied the title of 'Lord' to Jesus because it regarded him as the coming Judge. This is admittedly not impossible. If Jesus was regarded as the coming Son of man, and if this was a title which the early church did not itself use in referring to him, then it is conceivable that under the influence of Daniel 7:13 and possibly 1 Enoch 1:9 the early church gave to the coming Son of man the title of 'Lord'.[22] But this leaves unanswered the question as to why the early church regarded *Jesus* as this coming Son of man and Lord — a question all the more pressing for those who deny that Jesus spoke of himself as the coming Son of man. The answer to this question must surely be that the identification was confirmed (or created) as a result of the resurrection. The evidence that the early church regarded Jesus as the coming Judge because God had raised

him from the dead (Acts 17:31; 1 Thes. 1:10) probably reflects a primitive train of thought.

The point of this line of reasoning is that it indicates that the
resurrection of Jesus was understood as his exaltation to a
position of Lordship (Acts 2:36). The early church had no
reason to suppose that Jesus would return as Lord if he had
not been exalted by God. On the basis of the resurrection the
disciples may have argued that Jesus must be the coming Son
of man and therefore entitled to be called Lord in that connection, or that Jesus must be the exalted Lord, and therefore
the coming Lord and Son of man. The evidence suggests that
it was in fact the latter line of thought which was operative.

Hahn argues that Psalm 110:1, the source of the exaltation
motif, was originally applied to the parousia of Jesus (Mk.
14:61f.). At first, the resurrection of Jesus was regarded
simply as a withdrawal or translation to a state of inactivity
(Mk. 2:18-20; Acts 1:9-11; 3:20f.).[23] His argument has been
strongly criticized by Vielhauer, who notes that in the Old
Testament it is living people, not dead people, who are translated to heaven. The three texts cited in support of this
interpretation of Jesus' resurrection have been misinterpreted.
In Mark 14:61f. the reference is to a Son of man who is
*already* seated. The view that the transfer of the exaltation
from the parousia to the resurrection was a secondary stage
occasioned by the delay of the parousia and the need for
theological reformulation comes to grief on the fact that
intensive expectation of the parousia and belief in the present
exaltation of Jesus existed side by side in Paul's thought and
in all probability earlier. Nor was the thought of exaltation
developed solely on the basis of Psalm 110; it is found in
various contexts and with various backgrounds (Phil. 2:6-11;
Rom. 1:3f.), and the evidence suggests that it is a very early
conception. The life of the early church is unintelligible apart
from its belief in the exaltation of Jesus. Vielhauer concludes
— and coming from so radical a critic this statement is all
the more significant: 'The older view that the consciousness
of Jesus' exaltation arose as a result of the Easter appearances
remains standing as the more solidly based.'[24]

Hahn's case has also been examined in detail in a monograph

by W. Thüsing. He takes up the question whether the early church regarded salvation as essentially future or present, and proceeds to show that the early church was conscious in many ways of the present reality of salvation – and therefore of the present activity of Jesus. Jesus, therefore, is the living One. While it is true that references to his parousia are more explicit than references to his present exaltation, the two aspects of his work hang together, and the attempt to discover an earliest stage at which Jesus' activity was confined to the future is a failure. It was the resurrection appearances and the continued heavenly activity of Jesus which fanned the flame of hope in the parousia.[25]

Hahn has replied to his critics, but he has to admit the validity of several of Thüsing's arguments,[26] and there can be little doubt that his original case needs modification.

### The earliest Christian confession?

In his article on 'Maranatha' S. Schulz followed a hint of W. Bousset and W. Kramer that we should distinguish two different origins for the title 'Lord' in the New Testament. On the one hand, there is the title connected with the parousia and stemming from the Aramaic use of *mare* which has already been discussed. On the other hand, there is the application of the title *kyrios* in confessions of faith, and the writers listed argue that this developed quite independently in the Hellenistic Gentile church.[27] O. Cullmann has connected the development of the formula with the situation of persecution in which Christians affirmed the Lordship of Jesus over against the claims made by the emperor, and understands the use of the formula in 1 Corinthians 12:3 against this background; naturally he does₁ not regard this situation as the origin of the confession.[28] But, while the fact of persecution played an important role at a later date, it is very doubtful whether it is relevant at this early stage.[29] It is more plausible that Christian usage was influenced by Hellenistic cults in which the deities were known as 'lord' – and indeed the parallelism between Christian and pagan usage is explicitly noted by Paul (1 Cor. 8:5f.). So, for Bousset, the Lordship of Jesus came to be known by his disciples in an experience of worship similar to that in Hellenistic cults: 'During the day scattered, in the vocations of everyday life, in solitariness, within an alien world abandoned to scorn and contempt, they came together in the evening, probably as often as possible, for the common sacred meal. There they experienced the miracle of fellowship, the glow of the enthusiasm of a common faith and a common hope; there the spirit blazed high, and a world full of wonders surrounded them; prophets and those who speak in tongues, visionaries and ecstatic persons begin to speak; psalms, hymns, and spiritual songs sound through the room, the powers of brotherly kindness come alive in unexpected fashion; an unprecedented new life pulses through the throng of the Christians. And over this whole swaying sea of inspiration reigns the Lord Jesus as the head of his community, with his power immediately present in breathtaking palpable presence and certainty.' [30] So it is in Hellenistic worship that Jesus is known as the Lord. Kramer argues that in the phrase 'Jesus Christ is Lord' the use of 'Christ' as a name and not a title points to the Greek-speaking church as the origin of the phrase; it follows that the hymn in Philippians 2:6-11 arose in a Hellenistic setting. In the hymn the title is associated with Isaiah 45:23 LXX, and it thus emerges that LXX texts, originally referring to Yahweh, were applied in the Hellenistic church to Jesus.[31]

A number of questions arise as we consider this hypothesis. In the first place, the existence of two independent sources for the *kyrios* title, one in Aramaic usage and one in Greek cults, becomes doubtful as soon as we recognize that the primitive church regarded Jesus as Lord not only in respect of the parousia but also in respect of his present exaltation. It becomes possible that the confessional use of *kyrios* is rooted in Aramaic usage. Second, it is doubtful whether the confessional use of *kyrios* arose in the Greek-speaking church outside Palestine. For Kramer admits that the original use of the confessional formula was in relation to baptism, even if its use became more widespread; Bousset's view that it arose in Christian worship is thus to be rejected. Further, the formula is attested in the form 'Jesus is Lord' (without 'Christ') in 1 Corinthians 12:3 (the earliest literary example of the use). F. F. Bruce rightly affirms that an Aramaic-speaking Christian could equally well have said *Yesua' hu' mare*.[32] Third, the Gentile origin of the hymn in Philippians 2:6-11 is certainly to be rejected; it may be doubtful whether the hymn reflects an Aramaic original form, but its ideas are certainly Jewish rather than Gentile.[33]

The sum of these considerations makes it improbable that the confessional use of 'Lord' belongs to a later stage in Christology, and more likely that it arose at an early date. But what factors gave rise to this usage, and what content did the word have?

There can be no doubt that in the usage of the New Testament writers, beginning from Paul, the title of 'Lord' is regarded as the title used of God in the Old Testament and now applied to Jesus. Sometimes texts from the Old Testament which referred to Yahweh are applied to Jesus without the use of the word *kyrios* (1 Pet. 3:14f.), at other times the actual title is applied to Jesus (Rom. 10:13; Heb. 1:10; Jude 14f.; Rev. 17:14; 19:16; Phil. 2:9-11 does not use the title, but there can be no doubt that it is *kyrios* which is the 'name above every name'). Moreover, Jesus is thereby regarded as sharing the functions and the divine nature of God, as is evidenced by the application to him of the title 'Son of God' and even (in the latest writings) of 'God' itself. But was this the case at an earlier stage?

Here the contribution of K. Berger should be noted. He draws attention to the way in which the titles of God himself can be applied to his messengers. Evidence for this procedure is found in 3 Enoch, where Enoch is given lordship and receives the seventy names of God, since it is he who reveals the secrets of God. Similarly in the Samaritan source Memar Marqah Moses is clothed with the name of God on the basis of Exodus 23:20, and in Jewish sources angels are called 'lord'. On this basis Berger associates the use of divine titles with the revelation of God's messengers. So Jesus is acclaimed as 'Lord' when he is revealed as the one who is God's messenger and the one to whom the power of God's word and judgment have been given.[34] In this way Berger is able to ascribe the use of 'Lord' to Jewish Christianity (*i.e.* Hellenistic Jewish

Christianity), but at the cost of denying that originally 'Lord'
bore the connotation of divinity; the application of the title
to Jesus did not signify a breach with Judaism.

It will be obvious that this attractive theory has a number of
weaknesses, not the least of which is the question whether
a usage mainly attested in 3 Enoch and Memar Marqah can
have significantly affected the early Christians. It is also
doubtful whether the varied uses of 'Lord' for Jesus can have
flowed from one source; in particular, the usage in the Gospels
is wider than Berger allows. Nevertheless, Berger may have
indicated one influence which has contributed to the application of the title 'Lord' to Jesus within a Jewish setting.

It is notoriously difficult to say to what extent the early
Christians regarded Jesus as 'divine'. The word 'divine' is not
used in the New Testament in this context, and to have
asked an early Christian, 'Do you believe that Jesus is divine?'
would have been to use a category that was not part of his
thinking. To say that Jesus was Lord was, however, to ascribe
to him supreme authority under God, and to go beyond
anything that might be done on a merely literary level with a
figure of the past (like Moses or Enoch). It could not be
long before the ontological implications of such an affirmation
were realized, a process that was hastened by the belief that
Jesus was the Son of God. It is significant that by the time
of 1 Corinthians 8:6 Jesus is already regarded as participat-
ing in the task of creation and in Philippians 2:6-11 his pre-
existence is clearly evident. Here was another strand of
thought which contributed to the realization that he was
divine.[35]

To sum up: it is probable that the ascription of the title
'Lord' to Jesus was the product of various influences. The
understanding of him as Teacher and Lord during his ministry
was confirmed by the resurrection, which was understood as
God's vindication of him; Jesus was recognized as the living
one whose power was present in the church and who would
one day return as the exalted Son of man. When his career
was understood in the light of the Old Testament, his resurrection was understood in terms of Psalm 110:1 as an
exaltation to the right hand of God, and the title of Lord was

given a firm basis in the appellation used here. Increasingly the title was understood in terms of the Old Testament and regarded as an acknowledgment of a status equal to that of God the Father.

## NOTES

[1] See G. Quell and W. Foerster, *TDNT* III, pp. 1039-1095, for the basic facts. (W. Foerster also wrote *Herr ist Jesus* (1924) as a corrective to W. Bousset, *Kyrios Christos.*) Other discussions are O. Cullmann, *The Christology of the New Testament* (1959), pp. 195-237; F. Hahn, *The Titles of Jesus in Christology* (1969), ch. 2; R. H. Fuller, *The Foundations of New Testament Christology* (1965), pp. 50, 67f., 87-93, 119, 156-158, 184-186, 230f.; W. Kramer, *Christ, Lord, Son of God* (1966), pp. 65-107, 151-182; G. Vermes, *Jesus the Jew* (1973), pp. 103-128; S. Schulz, 'Maranatha und Kyrios Jesus', *ZNW* 53, 1962, pp. 125-144; F. F. Bruce, ' "Jesus is Lord" ', in J. M. Richards, *Soli Deo Gloria* (1968), pp. 23-36.

[2] W. Foerster, *TDNT* III, pp. 1050f.

[3] *Ibid.*

[4] W. Foerster *(TDNT* III, pp. 1054-1058) attempted to show that *kyrios* did not of itself connote the divinity of the emperor; subsequent writers (*e.g.* O. Cullmann, *op. cit.*, pp. 197-199) have given reason to question this theory.

[5] P. Vielhauer, *Aufsätze zum Neuen Testament* (1965), pp. 147-150. The Septuagintal evidence is given by W. G. Waddell, 'The Tetragrammaton in the LXX', *JTS* 45, 1944, pp. 158-161; S. Schulz, *art. cit.*, pp. 128-134.

[6] G. Dalman, *The Words of Jesus* (1909), pp. 324-327; *cf.* W. Bousset, *Kyrios Christos* (1913), p. 127; O. Cullmann, *op. cit.*, pp. 201f.

[7] J. A. Fitzmyer, 'The Contribution of Qumran Aramaic to the Study of the New Testament', *NTS* 20, 1973-74, pp. 386-391. The evidence is drawn from 1QapGen and 11QtgJob. Fitzmyer points out, however, that the use of *mare* as a translation of 'Yahweh' has not so far been attested. See further G. Vermes, *Jesus the Jew* (1973), pp. 111-122, for a wider survey of Jewish usage.

[8] S. Schulz, *art. cit.*, p. 137.

[9] W. Foerster, *TDNT* III, pp. 1086-1088.

[10] F. F. Bruce, ' "Jesus is Lord" ', in J. M. Richards, *Soli Deo Gloria* (1968), pp. 25f.

[11] We should not, however, overlook Jn. 13:13-16; 15:15, 20, where Jesus identifies himself as Teacher and Lord; this indicates the closeness of the terms in meaning, and shows that there is no difficulty in assuming that Jesus did use the terms with respect to himself. In Mt. 24:42 the 'master' in the parable has become 'your Lord', but this appears to be a piece of Matthaean elucidation (contrast Mk. 13:35; Lk. 12:40).

[12] P. Vielhauer, *Aufsätze zum Neuen Testament* (1965), pp. 150-157. There are certainly a number of instances in which the later Evangelists have substituted *kyrie* for other forms of address or simply inserted it

in their sources. But 'the double *kyrie* of Lk. 6:46; Mt. 7:21f., 25:11 is Semitic. At least the doubling is Semitic, and why should not the word be as well?' (W. Foerster, *TDNT* III, p. 1093).

[13] F. Hahn, *The Titles of Jesus in Christology* (1969), pp. 73-89.

[14] G. Vermes, *Jesus the Jew* (1973), pp. 122-127.

[15] Vermes adopts inferior textual evidence in Mk. 1:40; 9:22; 10:51 to obtain examples of his theory.

[16] W. Foerster, *TDNT* III, pp. 1093f. The authority of Jesus over his disciples is especially brought out by K. H. Rengstorf, *TDNT* IV, pp. 444-455.

[17] The basic treatment is K. G. Kuhn, *TDNT* IV, pp. 466-472. Kuhn rules out the possibility of a prophetic perfect, but it is defended by M. Black, 'The Maranatha invocation and Jude 14, 15 (1 Enoch 1:9)', in B. Lindars and S. S. Smalley (eds.), *Christ and Spirit in the New Testament* (1973), pp. 189-196.

[18] See O. Cullmann's description of Bousset's contortions in successive works (*The Christology of the New Testament* (1959), pp. 213f.). *Cf.* W. Bousset, *Kyrios Christos* (1970), p. 129; R. Bultmann, *Theology of the New Testament* (1952), I, p. 52.

[19] M. Black, *art. cit.* It must be underlined that the crucial Aramaic words are not preserved in the fragment, and the Greek fragment of the passage has 'he (*sc.* God) comes'. Black admits that it is unlikely that *kyrios* (Jude 14) represents the original wording.

[20] R. Bultmann, *op. cit.* P. Vielhauer (*Aufsätze zum Neuen Testament* (1965), p. 159) claims that this interpretation cannot be excluded.

[21] F. Hahn, *The Titles of Jesus in Christology* (1969), pp. 89-103, quotation from p. 102.

[22] W. Kramer, *Christ, Lord, Son of God* (1966), pp. 99-103.

[23] F. Hahn, *op. cit.*, pp. 129-135.

[24] P. Vielhauer, *op. cit.*, pp. 167-175. It should be noted that Vielhauer's criticism of Hahn often involves assigning a *later* date to the relevant texts which Hahn assigns to the earliest church. But his objections by no means rest exclusively on this dating, and his points regarding the interpretation of the texts are often well taken.

[25] W. Thüsing, *Erhöhungsvorstellung und Parusieerwartung in der ältesten nachösterlichen Christologie* (1969).

[26] F. Hahn, 'Methodenprobleme einer Christologie des Neuen Testaments', *Verkündigung und Forschung* 2, 1970, pp. 3-41, especially pp. 35-38.

[27] S. Schulz, 'Maranatha und Kyrios Jesus', *ZNW* 53, 1962, pp. 126f.; *cf.* W. Bousset, *Kyrios Christos* (1970), p. 151; W. Kramer, *Christ, Lord, Son of God* (1966), pp. 103-105. Similarly, P. Vielhauer, *op. cit.*, p. 167.

[28] O. Cullmann, *The Christology of the New Testament* (1959), pp. 218-220.

[29] W. Kramer, *op. cit.*, pp. 65f.

[30] W. Bousset, *op. cit.*, p. 135.

[31] W. Kramer, *op. cit.*, pp. 67f.

[32] F. F. Bruce, ' "Jesus is Lord" ', in J. M. Richards, *Soli Deo Gloria* (1968), pp. 23f.

[33] R. P. Martin, *Carmen Christi* (1967), pp. 297-299.

[34] K. Berger, 'Zum traditionsgeschichtlichen Hintergrund christologischer

Hoheitstitel', *NTS* 17, 1970-71, pp. 391-425, especially pp. 413-422.

[35] On this theme see especially R. G. Hamerton-Kelly, *Pre-Existence, Wisdom and the Son of Man* (1973).

# 7 IF YOU ARE THE SON OF GOD

Certainly Jesus did not take up the challenge of Satan to turn stones into bread or to jump from the pinnacle of the temple in order to demonstrate that he was the Son of God, and Satan himself might have been tempted to wonder whether he thought of himself in this way at all. But whatever Satan may have thought, there have certainly been modern scholars who have questioned whether Jesus thought of himself as the Son of God and whether the earliest church thought of him in this way. In a useful brief survey of the title R. Schnackenburg has carefully listed the current opinions among scholars and suggests that four approaches can be seen.[1] First, there is the conservative approach which holds that Jesus used the title in a Messianic sense and referred to himself as the unique Son of God. Second, there is the religio-historical explanation of the title in terms of the Hellenistic concept of the divine man (*theios anēr*)[2] with influence from the Gnostic myth.[3] Third, in various ways scholars have used critical methods to establish some kind of starting-point in the teaching of Jesus for the later development in the church. For example, behind the title, as found in the baptismal narrative, J. Jeremias has traced an original 'servant' terminology which was reinterpreted in terms of sonship.[4] Others link the use of the title for the Davidic Messiah with Jesus' own consciousness of a filial relation to God and so account for the church's use.[5] Or again Jesus' view that he was a son of God in the sense in which all men (or all good men) are sons of God was developed by the church into an assertion of uniqueness.[6] Fourth, there is the traditio-historical approach which accounts for all the uses of the title within the developing theology of the early church; on this view either we do not know how Jesus thought of himself, or he is to be regarded as a charismatic man of God and prophet.[7]

This rapid listing indicates several possible (and impossible) solutions to the problem. It emerges that the key questions are: first, whether Jesus thought of himself in terms of divine Sonship, and, if so, what was the meaning he attached to it; or whether he was conscious of some other role as a result of which it was natural for the early church to regard him as the Son of God. Second, were there any external influences which led to the introduction of the title in the early church or to significant modification of its use? Third, can we formulate a history of the use of the title in the church? We shall not be able to organize our discussion strictly in terms of these three questions, but they may serve to keep clear the issues that will arise.

### Possible influences on Jesus and the early church

It is natural to look in the Old Testament and Judaism for the primary influences upon New Testament thinking, especially because time and again Old Testament texts are quoted with reference to the divine Sonship of Jesus and of Christians. The Old Testament refers to three types of people as sons of God. The term is applied to angels and other heavenly beings, but this has not influenced Christology.[8] Second, it is applied to Israel as a whole to express the relationship into which they had been brought to God by his covenant with them. To a limited extent this relationship was predicated of individuals who were conscious of God's fatherly care for them and who served him obediently. Most important for our present interest, the term was applied to the king who is regarded as standing in a special relationship (on behalf of his people) to God. Scholarship is agreed that this usage does not reflect the Egyptian idea of the physical generation of the king by a god, but rather stands close to the Babylonian view in which the king was simply given a lofty status; the relationship was one of divine care and protection and human service and obedience. Of particular importance is the expression of the relationship in 2 Samuel 7:14; Psalm 2:7 and Psalm 89:27f. with reference to David and his successors.

In Judaism there was a tendency to drop the first use of the term in the interests of a firmly defined monotheism, but the other two uses continued. The thought of God as the Father of his people was developed and increasingly personalized. This is especially obvious in the Hellenistically orientated book of Wisdom which is being increasingly recognized as significant for New Testament thought. Here the just man is seen as God's son and he puts his trust in God to help him in the midst of persecution; his trust is rewarded with the hope of immortality (Wisdom 2:10-20; 5:1-5).

The case with regard to the use of the term of a 'Messianic' figure is not so clear. Older books cite 1 Enoch 105:2; 4 Ezra 7:28f.; 13:32, 37, 52 and 14:9 as evidence, but these references rest on a late text (in the first case) and on mistranslations of the word 'servant' (in the other cases).[9] However, it is now possible to cite some evidence from Qumran. In 4Q Florilegium there is a citation of 2 Samuel 7:14 with reference to the Davidic Messiah. The way was thus opened up for a description of the Messiah as the Son of God. In another passage, which unfortunately is fragmentary, there is a possible reference to God's begetting of the Messiah, as in Psalm 2:7 (1Q28a 2:11f.), but this is far from certain.[10] In a third passage, which is not yet officially published, there is a reference to somebody who 'shall be hailed (as) the Son of God, and they shall call him Son of the Most High'; here we have Aramaic parallels to the terminology used in Luke 1:32, 35 of Jesus.[11] It would be rash to offer any verdict on this text (4QpsDan A$^a$) until further light has been shed on it by the experts, but we have at least sufficient evidence to support R. H. Fuller's statement that 'Son of God was *just coming into use* as a Messianic title in pre-Christian Judaism'.[12]

Outside Judaism the idea of divine Sonship was also to be found in Hellenistic sources. But the most recent survey of the topic, by W. von Martitz,[13] emphasizes that this idea was not so widespread as is often supposed, and that the actual term is used comparatively infrequently. In particular, it was not a standard epithet of the so-called 'divine man' (*theios anēr* — a phrase which is not in fact used in the sources but is the creation of modern scholarship).[14] This is an important corrective to the views of earlier scholars such as G. P. Wetter and L. Bieler, from whose works one might gain the impression that 'divine men' proclaiming 'I am the Son of God' could be heard at every street corner.[15]

One further point needs to be cleared up before we turn to the meaning of the terms in the New Testament. F. Hahn makes the point that in reality we have two different titles to deal with here: 'the Son' and 'Son of God' must be carefully distinguished from each other, since they have different origins, although in the later New Testament documents they were (not surprisingly) assimilated to each other. When we ask how we may distinguish between the occurrence of these two titles, Hahn's answer is that the former title is used absolutely without the addition 'of God', and the latter is never used in conjunction with the term 'Father'.[16] Hahn's distinction has been generally accepted,[17] but it is of questionable validity. First, the distinction was not perceived by John or by Mark, the latter of whom regards 'the Son' (Mk. 13:32) as equivalent to the 'Son of God' used elsewhere in his Gospel. Second, when the forms 'his Son' or 'my Son' occur, it is not always clear whether 'God' or 'the Father' is the antecedent.[18] Third, there are cases where 'Son of God' is used in conjunction with 'the Father'.[19] These points make it highly unlikely that there was a basic distinction between two different titles in the New Testament use of 'son'.

### The filial consciousness of Jesus

In an earlier section we have referred to the substantial evidence that Jesus used the term *'Abba'* as an expression of the relationship between God and himself.[20] But did Jesus use the correlative term 'son' in any special way with regard to himself, and did other people use it during his lifetime? Our experience with the titles discussed earlier does not lead us to expect that Jesus would have proclaimed such a self-claim from the housetops, and the evidence confirms this expectation. The decisive text is Matthew 11:27 (Lk. 10:22). There are basically two approaches to the interpretation of the text. On the one hand, there are those who follow E. Norden and R. Bultmann in finding Hellenistic thought expressed in the text: the mutual knowledge of father and son is typical of Hellenistic mysticism and has nothing to do with the historical Jesus.[21] Most recently the proponents of this approach find the background to the text in Hellenistic Judaism and specifically in speculations regarding the character of wisdom. The saying belongs to the latest phase of development of the Q material.[22] On the other hand, there is the lonely voice of J. Jeremias who points to the undeniable Palestinian language of the saying with its circumlocution to express a reciprocal relationship: 'only a father and a son know each other, and therefore only a son can reveal a father'. He further observes that what we have here is a statement of a generic relationship, true of any father-son relationship; the term 'the Father' is not used as a title for God in Aramaic, and hence the correlative 'the son' is not used as a title either.[23] A detailed discussion of these two approaches is not possible here, but in our view the evidence favours the second view.[24] Note, however, what is involved. 'Son' does not function here as a title; it occurs within a statement of what is generally true. But (a point overlooked by Jeremias), since 'a father' in the metaphor undoubtedly refers to God, Jesus is applying 'a son' to himself, and is thus making an implicit claim to a unique relationship with God. If 'son' is not a *title* of Jesus here, it is at least a description of his relation to God.

Two other texts may also refer to Jesus in this way. The first is the allusion to the son of the owner of the vineyard in Mark 12:6. Here again the authenticity of the text is vigorously challenged on the grounds that *a.* 'son' was not a recognized current Messianic title, and *b.* the parable looks like an allegorical construction by a church for whom Jesus was already known as the Son of God who was slain by the Jews.[25] The former of these two points is irrelevant: it is doubtful whether Jesus would have used a current Messianic title to refer openly to himself (in the case of Mt. 11:27 we are dealing with private instruction to his disciples). Jeremias rightly observes that we must distinguish between what Jesus himself meant and what the audience may have taken from his words. [26] The second point is stronger, but J. D. M. Derrett has shown how naturally the term 'son' can be accounted for *within the parabolic framework*,[27] and hence the probability that the term represents early church allegorization is considerably reduced.

The case with the other saying is not so clear. In Mark 13:32 the date of the last day is known to no-one, 'not even the angels in heaven, nor the Son, but only the Father'. The standard argument in defence of this saying is that nobody in the early church would have invented such a 'hard saying' in which the Son is made to confess his ignorance.[28] The force of this argument is weakened by the claim that the words 'nor the Son, but only the Father' belong to a stage at which it was necessary to underline the ignorance of Jesus over against apocalyptic enthusiasts who were sure that *they* knew the date. Further, the absolute use of the terms 'the Son' and 'the Father' speaks against an Aramaic origin for this part of the verse.[29] It is difficult, therefore, to be sure that this saying goes back to Jesus in its present form.

The evidence for Jesus' use of the word 'Son' with reference to himself is thus slight, and the weight falls on Matthew 11:27. It ties in, however, with other uses in the Gospels. Thus Jesus is addressed by the heavenly voice at his baptism as 'my Son', and he is similarly designated in the transfiguration story (Mk. 1:11; 9:7). The widely held view that in these texts 'son' has replaced an original 'servant' as a result of a reinterpretation of the Greek word *pais* is not upheld by the evidence, at least in our opinion.[30] So the view that one root of the church's understanding of Jesus as 'the Son' was a development of an earlier 'servant' Christology lacks foundation. Two other main sources for the use of the title here have been suggested. The one is Psalm 2:7, where 'son' was interpreted by the early church as an address by God to the Messiah. Hence, it has been argued, the use of 'Son' for Jesus rests on the earlier equation of Jesus with the Messiah.[31] This is possible, but in the baptismal narrative the line of thought appears to be that Jesus is the Messiah *because* he is the Son of God, rather than vice versa. The other possible source is Abraham/Isaac typology (Gn. 22:2, 12, 16), [32] and, if established, this would confirm that the thought of a personal relationship is present.

Jesus is also addressed as 'Son of God' by the demons which he cast out (Mk. 3:11; 5:7) and by Satan (Mt. 4:3, 6). This feature is often associated with the idea of the 'divine man' who has supernatural powers and is to be regarded as the Son of God. It should, however, be noted that in the temptation story Jesus refuses to do the things that are associated by the devil with the title 'Son of God': he will not act as a wonder-working Son of God. And the use of the title by demons need not be a sign of Hellenistic influence; it was possible in Palestine, where men conscious of demon possession would regard an exorcist as standing in a special relationship to God.

We have argued that the use of 'Son' in the Gospels reflects the filial consciousness of Jesus, which is also expressed in his use of 'Father' to refer to God. That such a consciousness is expressed in terms of Jewish concepts has been argued independently by G. Vermes and K. Berger. The former draws attention to the way in which Jewish saints and teachers could be addressed by God as 'my son' – and this heavenly voice could be heard by demons. Vermes concludes from this background that it is quite possible that Jesus was called Son of God in view of his activities as a worker of miracles and an exorcist and his consciousness of intimate contact with God. [33] The latter notes how God is regarded as the Father of wisdom and of the messengers of wisdom who know him and his secrets. The title of Son thus refers to Jesus primarily as the messenger of God who possesses true knowledge of him. [34] Both of these contributions shed light on the essentially Jewish character of the concept of Sonship in the Gospels. The question may be raised whether their effect is not to minimize the uniqueness of Jesus; in fact, however, there is an exclusiveness about the claims of Jesus which shows that his relation to God is regarded as unique. In this consciousness of his filial relation to God lies the basis of his mission, which is formulated in terms of uniqueness.

### 'Son of God' in the early church

According to Hahn and Fuller the title 'Son of God' was first applied to Jesus in the early Palestinian church with reference to his future work as Messiah and only at a later stage (Hellenistic Jewish Christianity) was it applied to him with reference to his exalted position after the resurrection.[35] We have already seen that this thesis is weakly based in respect of the other titles which are regarded as being used originally in connection with the parousia, and examination shows that the same is true in the present instance. Hahn's basic evidence for his view is to be found in Luke 1:32f.; Mark 14:61f. and 1 Thessalonians 1:9f. which testify to the Palestinian view, and in Romans 1:3f.; Acts 13:33; Hebrews 1:5; 5:5; Colossians 1:13 and 1 Corinthians 15:25-28 which testify to the Hellenistic view. These texts will not bear the burden of proof. There is nothing to show that the first three texts cited offer us the *earliest* use of the title in the Palestinian church, and the first two of them are too vague in expression to show decisively that 'Son of God' was a title expressly connected with the parousia. In the case of 1 Thessalonians 1:9f., it must be noted that the text expressly refers to the resurrection of Jesus as the guarantee of his· future coming, and that nothing suggests that Jesus becomes 'Son of God' in connection with his future work; there is some doubt whether the text, which is to be regarded as a pre-Pauline fragment, did not originally refer to the Son of man as the one expected from heaven.[36] It is significant that Fuller rejects these texts as evidence, and he bases his case on Romans 1:3f. instead. This text has long been recognized as a pre-Pauline formula elaborated by Paul, but there is no agreement regarding the precise wording of the original formula, although it must have contained at least the words 'who was made of the seed of David . . . who was designated Son of God by resurrection from the dead'.[37] Fuller argues that this means that Jesus was foreordained to be the Son of God at the parousia, and cites as parallels to this thought Acts 10:42; 17:31 and 3:20. But this is a most unnatural reading of the text in Romans, and the parallels cited do not prove the point; the first two are concerned with the foreordination of

Jesus to be Judge, but judgment is not specifically an attribute of the Son of God, and the third text, as we have seen earlier, does not mean that Jesus will become Christ only at the parousia. Fuller's case is no more plausible than Hahn's.

We are left, therefore, with the texts that show that divine Sonship was linked with the resurrection. By raising him from the dead God declared him to be his Son. The passages cited by Hahn as testifying to the thought of the Hellenistic church come in as evidence at this point. Whether it is appropriate to call them 'Hellenistic Jewish' is, however, another question, since we have argued that this rigid schematization of thought does not do justice to the flexibility of the early church. It must be admitted that we do not know exactly when and where the title came into use in the early church, although we can be confident that it belongs to Jewish Christianity. The earliest reference to its use is in Acts 9:20, where it is distinctive of the preaching of Paul; this may suggest that it was not used in the very earliest period of the church, but little weight can be placed on such speculation.

Granted that the title was used in this way with reference to the resurrection, a second problem is that of its significance. Many scholars argue that its use suggests that the early church thought of Jesus as becoming Son of God from the resurrection onwards. Sometimes this view is called 'adoptionist',[38] but the use of this term, taken over from later Christological controversies in the sub-apostolic church, is anachronistic and misleading.[39] What is envisaged is a new functional status in which Jesus is accorded the position of Son of God with all its rights and powers. On this view 'Son of David' in the formula in Romans 1:3f. is held to have been an expression of the lower status which Jesus had during his earthly life; in this way the formula can be held to testify to a 'two-stage' Christology in which the resurrection effects a decisive change in Jesus' status. Only at a later date (on this view) did the early church come to regard 'Son of God' as an ontological title, expressive of the 'nature' of Jesus, and to regard it as an appropriate title for him in the period before his resurrection.

Our question, accordingly, is whether the evidence supports this view that the early church dated the Sonship of Jesus from his resurrection. May it not be the case that the early church regarded the resurrection as a confirmation of an already-existent status rather than as the conferring of a new status? We would suggest that this is a more accurate exegesis of the relevant texts. With regard to Romans 1:3f. it is highly unlikely that one who was regarded as 'Son of David' (a Messianic title) before his death should have been adopted by God as his Son at a subsequent stage; what the resurrection did was to declare with power his real status. It confirmed and manifested an existing position. Similarly, the use of Psalm 2:7 in Acts 13:33 does not mean that God raised up Jesus and so made him his Son. It is more probable that we should see the line of thought in Wisdom 2:13-18. Here the enemies of the righteous man acknowledge that 'He professes to have knowledge of God, and calls himself a child of the Lord . . . and boasts that God is his father'. So they resolve to test his claims: 'Let us see if his words are true, and let us test what will happen at the end of his life; for if the righteous man is God's son, he will help him, and will deliver him from the hand of his adversaries.' In the same way Psalm 2:7 can be fittingly applied to the risen Jesus because the resurrection proved that he, a just and righteous man (Acts 13:28), was treated as the Son of God by being raised from the dead; the 'begetting' in the text obviously refers metaphorically to the new life in the re-surrection and not to any initiation of divine Sonship. Indeed, if we ask what prompted the early church to apply Psalm 2:7 to the resurrection, it seems extremely unlikely that it was read as an allusion to the resurrection and then applied to Jesus; it is much more likely that the mention of the Lord's anointed and his Son led to the application to Jesus and then to his resurrection. The use of the psalm thus pre-supposes that the early church had already formed an estimate of Jesus as the Messiah or Son of God.

If our arguments are valid, they show that the resurrection was not regarded as the moment at which Jesus became the Son of God. On the contrary, the resurrection was a confir-mation of his existing position and status. This leads us to probe further backwards into another area of thought.

Our third problem, therefore, is the application of the title to the pre-existence of Jesus. Here we are indebted especially to W. Kramer for his careful isolation of a set of early formulae in which the title of Son of God is associated with the pre-existence of Jesus. He draws attention to Galatians 4:4f.; John 3:17; 1 John 4:9, 10, 14 and Romans 8:3 as witnesses to a formula that God sent his Son, a formula which presupposes his pre-existence. Kramer also thinks that formulae about God 'giving up' his Son (*paradidōmi*) referred originally to the coming of the Son of God into the world in a broad sense and were not limited to the thought of his death (Rom. 8:32; Jn. 3:16; Gal. 2:20; Eph. 5:2, 25; Rom. 4:25), but this is more speculative.[40] In any case it is beyond question that the concept of pre-existence was already in use before the time of Paul to signify the lofty status of Jesus.

The origins of this type of thinking need some investigation. R. Bultmann claims that the idea of sonship developed in the Hellenistic church under the influence of ideas of divine men who claimed to be sons of a god, son-divinities worshipped in the mystery religions, and the figure of the redeemer in the Gnostic myth.[41] This understanding of the situation is open to considerable doubt. So far as pre-existence is concerned, only the last of these influences is relevant; the first two are linked more with the question of the divinity of Jesus during his lifetime. But it needs to be insisted, however tedious it may be to continue to repeat the old answer to the equally tedious assertion of the point in question, that there is still no evidence for dating the Gnostic myth of a redeemer who comes down from heaven before the rise of Christian faith in the coming of Jesus into the world. Such evidence may at some time be produced; there have been hints that some of the Nag-Hammadi Gnostic documents (none of which were written in the first century) may contain evidence of non-Christian testimony to the existence of the Gnostic myth, but this evidence has still to be produced.[42] Even if such testimony is produced, it has still to be shown that it influenced Christian thought. But this is unlikely, because the Christian thought in question is basically Jewish in expression. It is much more probable that the nearest parallel to

Christian thought is to be found in Jewish speculation about the figure of wisdom as the pre-existent agent of God in creation who comes and dwells among men.[43]

Such a manner of thinking is usually associated with 'Hellenistic Jewish' thinking, since it occurs primarily in Greek documents such as Wisdom and the writings of Philo, although the clear presence of teaching about the pre-existence of wisdom in Sirach 24 (originally written in Hebrew) urges caution here. In the New Testament an important expression of the idea is to be found in the hymn in Philippians 2:6-11 which, as we have seen, is Jewish in thought rather than Gentile. It is difficult to be more specific about the rise of this concept in the early church, but at the least we can affirm that it arose in Jewish Christianity and had become a fixed part of early Christian formulae well before the composition of Paul's letters.

The relation of this idea to that of the conception of Jesus by the Spirit is one that deserves some attention. The stories of the birth of Jesus relate his divine Sonship to his conception by the Spirit and show that he was to be regarded as the Son of God during his earthly life. Here divine Sonship is clearly a characteristic of his nature and not simply an expression of function or status. The development of this concept is commonly regarded as coming at a fairly late stage in Christology and as being, strictly speaking, incompatible with the idea of pre-existence. Both Hahn and Fuller, however, accept the conclusion of M. Dibelius that the story of the virgin birth has a background in Hellenistic Jewish thought rather than in pagan thought, and this is undoubtedly correct.[44] This is, of course, a long way from saying that the story is historical, and most scholars would argue that it is a theological expression of the supreme status to be assigned to Jesus; it is, like pre-existence, an expression of the fact that Jesus is an expression of the saving purpose of God. We may well want to assess the historicity of the stories otherwise, but this is not the place for a discussion of this intricate issue.[45] The thought of pre-existence is not explicitly raised in the birth stories, but the judgment that it is incompatible with them is faulty; the two concepts of pre-existence and conception by the Spirit are complementary and arise from two different types of language which are simply laid side by side in the New Testament without any consciousness that they are incompatible.

With the use of 'Son of God' we thus encounter a title in which the relation of Jesus to God is especially prominent and in which the concept of deity is present. It took time for the full implications of this title to be worked out by the church. That it was connected originally with Jesus' own estimate of himself is highly probable; what the early church did was to draw out the implications of his filial consciousness, as it was confirmed by the resurrection and illuminated by Old Testament prophecy and contemporary Jewish thought about the figure of wisdom. The pagan centurion may not have realized fully what he meant when he affirmed, 'Truly this man was the Son of God!' (Mk. 15:39): the early church came to an increasing recognition of all that the title meant, so that in the end it was seen that it was not inappropriate to call Jesus 'God'.[46]

# NOTES

[1] R. Schnackenburg, in *Lexicon für Theologie und Kirche* (1964), IX, cols. 851-854. For this chapter see J. Bienock, *Sohn Gottes als Christusbezeichnung der Synoptiker* (1951); O. Cullmann, *The Christology of the New Testament* (1959), pp. 270-305; F. Hahn, *The Title of Jesus in Christology* (1969), pp. 279-333; B. M. F. van Iersel, *'Der Sohn' in den Synoptischen Jesusworten*[2] (1964); R. H. Fuller, *The Foundations of New Testament Christology* (1965), pp. 31-33, 65, 68-72, 114f., 164-167, 187f., 192-197, 231f.; W. Kramer, *Christ, Lord, Son of God* (1966), pp. 108-128, 183-194; E. Schweizer *et al.*, *TDNT* VIII, pp. 334-397; G. Vermes, *Jesus the Jew* (1973), pp. 192-222. Some of the material is presented more fully in my two earlier articles: 'The Divine Sonship of Jesus', *Interpretation* 21, 1967, pp. 87-103; 'The Development of Christology in the Early Church', *Tyn.B* 18, 1967, pp. 77-93.

[2] W. Bousset, *Kyrios Christos* (1970), pp. 91-98.

[3] *Cf.* R. Bultmann, *Theology of the New Testament* (1952), I, pp. 128-133; but Bultmann also recognizes that at first 'Son of God' was used as a royal title for the Messiah (*op. cit.*, p. 50).

[4] J. Jeremias, *New Testament Theology* (1971), I, pp. 53-55; *cf. TDNT* V, pp. 701f.

[5] O. Cullmann, *op.cit.*; B. M. F. van Iersel, *op. cit.*

[6] A view attributed to W. Grundmann by O. Cullmann (*op. cit.*, pp.

275f.), but later repudiated by that scholar. (See W. Grundmann, 'Sohn Gottes (ein Diskussionsbeitrag)', *ZNW* 47, 1956, pp. 113-133, especially p. 130 n. 38.)

[7] R. Bultmann, *op. cit.*; F. Hahn, *op. cit.*, pp. 313f., 372ff.

[8] Heb. 1:5-14 rejects the idea that angels are on a level with the Son.

[9] It is not clear whether Christian influence is present in T. Levi 18:6.

[10] E. Lohse, *TDNT* VIII, p. 361.

[11] J. A. Fitzmyer, 'The Contribution of Qumran Aramaic to the Study of the New Testament', *NTS* 20, 1973-74, pp. 382-407, especially pp. 391-394.

[12] R. H. Fuller, *The Foundations of New Testament Christology* (1965), p. 32. The usage in Philo (who regarded the Logos as the elder son of God) cannot be discussed here.

[13] W. von Martitz, *TDNT* VIII, pp. 335-340.

[14] W. von Martitz (*op. cit.*, p. 338 n. 23) says that *theios* was used predicatively, not as an attribute.

[15] G. P. Wetter, *Der Sohn Gottes* (1916); L. Bieler, $\theta EIO\Sigma$ ANHP, *das Bild des 'göttlichen Menschen' in Spätantike und Frühchristentum* (1935-36).

[16] F. Hahn, *The Titles of Jesus in Christology* (1969), pp. 279f.

[17] P. Vielhauer, *Aufsätze zum Neuen Testament* (1965), pp. 194f.; E. Schweizer, *TDNT* VIII, p. 370 n. 258. Schweizer refers to the discussion by B. M. F. van Iersel, *'Der Sohn' in den synoptischen Jesusworten*[2] (1964), pp. 173-184. Van Iersel shows that Jesus did not use the title 'Son of God' or link the associations of that title with his own relationship to God as his Son, but he argues that the church's development of the title rests on Jesus' own statements, and in the appendix to his book (pp. 190f.) he criticizes Hahn's statement of an absolute distinction between the two usages.

[18] See Mk. 1:11; 9:7; 12:6; Gal. 1:16; Col. 1:13.

[19] See Gal. 4:6; Eph. 4:6, 13; 1 Jn. 4:14f.; Rev. 2:18, 27. *Cf.* my article in *Interpretation* 21, 1967, pp. 87f.

[20] See above, p. 46.

[21] R. Bultmann, *The History of the Synoptic Tradition*[2] (1968), pp. 159f.

[22] S. Schulz, *Q – die Spruchquelle der Evangelisten* (1972), pp. 213-228.

[23] J. Jeremias, *New Testament Theology* (1971), I, pp. 56-61; *cf.* T. W. Manson, *The Sayings of Jesus* (1949), pp. 78-80.

[24] F. Hahn (*The Titles of Jesus in Christology* (1969), pp. 308-311) also regards the thought as based on the Old Testament, but apparently ascribes the saying to the Jewish church.

[25] W. G. Kümmel, *Promise and Fulfilment* (1957), pp. 82f.

[26] J. Jeremias, *The Parables of Jesus*[2] (1963), pp. 72f.

[27] J. D. M. Derrett, *Law in the New Testament* (1970), pp. 286-312.

[28] B. M. F. van Iersel, *'Der Sohn' in den synoptischen Jesusworten*[2] (1964), pp. 117-123.

[29] R. Pesch, *Naherwartungen* (1968), pp. 190-194. *Cf.* J. Jeremias, *New Testament Theology* (1971), I, p. 131 n. 1.

[30] I. H. Marshall, 'Son of God or Servant of Yahweh? – A Reconsideration of Mark I.11', *NTS* 15, 1968-69, pp. 326-336. See, however, O.

Cullmann, *The Christology of the New Testament* (1959), p. 66; J. Jeremias, *TDNT* V, pp. 701f.

[31] E. Schweizer, *TDNT* VIII, pp. 367f.

[32] E. Best, *The Temptation and the Passion* (1965), pp. 169f.

[33] G. Vermes, *Jesus the Jew* (1973), pp. 206-210.

[34] K. Berger, 'Zum traditionsgeschichtlichen Hintergrund Christologischer Hoheitstitel', *NTS* 17, 1970-71, p. 391-426, especially pp. 422-424.

[35] F. Hahn, *The Titles of Jesus in Christology* (1969), pp. 284-288; R. H. Fuller, *The Foundations of New Testament Christology* (1965), pp. 164-167.

[36] E. Schweizer, *TDNT* VIII, p. 370.

[37] R. H. Fuller, *op. cit.*, pp. 165f.; *cf.* W. Kramer, *Christ, Lord, Son of God* (1966), pp. 108f.; also J. D. G. Dunn, 'Jesus — Flesh and Spirit: An Exposition of Romans 1:3-4', *JTS* n.s. 24, 1973, pp. 40-68.

[38] W. Kramer, *op. cit.*, pp. 108-111.

[39] E. Schweizer, *TDNT* VIII, pp. 366f.

[40] W. Kramer, *op. cit.*, pp. 111-123.

[41] R. Bultmann, *Theology of the New Testament* (1952), I, p. 130.

[42] For the hints see J. M. Robinson, 'The Coptic Gnostic Library Today', *NTS* 14, 1967-68, pp. 356-401, especially pp. 373-380.

[43] This influence is noted by R. Bultmann, *op. cit.*, p. 132, See E. Schweizer, *Neotestamentica* (1963), pp. 105-109; *TDNT* VIII, pp. 374-376.

[44] F. Hahn, *The Titles of Jesus in Christology* (1969), pp. 295-298; R. H. Fuller, *The Foundations of New Testament Christology* (1965), pp. 195f.; *cf.* M. Dibelius, *Botschaft und Geschichte* (1953), I, pp.1-78.

[45] Still highly relevant is J. G. Machen, *The Virgin Birth of Christ* (1958).

[46] A. W. Wainwright, 'The Confession "Jesus is God" in the New Testament', *SJT* 10, 1957, pp. 274-299; and *The Trinity in the New Testament* (1962); *cf.* O. Cullmann, *The Christology of the New Testament* (1959), pp. 306-314. Other discussions of 'Son of God' include P. Pokorny, *Der Gottessohn* (1971); M. Hengel, *The Son of God* (1976).

# 8 AN UNFINISHED TASK

It is the inherent danger of the 'survey' type of book that it leaves its readers with a set of simple generalizations which they may be tempted to accept as the definitive word on the subject without going over the material for themselves so as to see the surveyor's remarks in context and to judge whether they fairly summarize the situation. To some extent this is a necessary occupational hazard; nowadays the volume of knowledge in any given subject is so great that no one person can encompass it all. We must all be dependent on the summaries of experts in each small area. At the same time, nobody who wishes to have a first-hand knowledge of a particular area can hope to achieve it by remaining content with the summary.

It is worth while to make this rather trite comment at this point, because we are acutely aware of the limitations of the present survey. It has confined itself to one particular approach, the titles of Jesus, and to one particular historical period, the pre-Pauline era. Within this area much has been left untouched. There are titles (such as 'Son of David' and 'Servant of Yahweh') which have been almost totally ignored Those that have been discussed have been treated cursorily. Outside the area the gaps are even greater. We have ignored the whole question of early confessions, hymns and similar stereotyped material from the early church.[1] We have paid no attention to the thought of Paul or any of the other New Testament writers as such. We have had to pass over the increasingly important question of the hypothetical

Christology of the hypothetical community which produced the hypothetical document 'Q'.[2] Another glaring omission is the question of John's Gospel, and the value of the teaching it contains (especially on 'Son of man' and 'Son of God') as evidence for the mind of Jesus himself and the community in which the teaching was known and preserved.[3] A survey of the whole problem by another writer might appear very different from the present one.[4]

These are the limitations imposed by the vastness of the subject. A further limitation is due to the amount of controversy which surrounds the subject. At the outset we argued for a stance which is not shared by many of the principal students in the area. We claimed that the indirect evidence supported the view that Jesus had a Christology, and we criticized the assumption that the thought of the early church can be analysed in terms of Palestinian, Hellenistic Jewish and Hellenistic Gentile components. Throughout our survey we have found ourselves not simply reporting opinions but attempting, however briefly, to analyse them and criticize them from our particular point of view. We hope that this will make the book more useful to the reader than a mere chronicle of points of view. But it does mean that the reader must be prepared to go over the material for himself and weigh up the arguments on both sides.

Finally, the scale of the treatment has made it impossible to get down to the detailed exegesis and scrutiny of texts on which all theological and historical constructions must rest. General considerations about what Jesus might or might not have said are no substitute for examination of the actual sayings attributed to him, a task which is clearly beyond the scope of a broad survey. But there can be no substitute for such detailed work if we are to arrive at an understanding of the New Testament based on firm foundations.

All this makes it impossible for us to offer a definitive picture of the development of Christology. It will be remembered that at the outset we uttered a prophecy to this effect; the reader may be assured that here, if anywhere, he is confronted by a genuine *vaticinium ante eventum* — which has truly come to pass.[5] It has not proved possible to offer a reconstruction of the history of early Christology, although it has been possible to show the inadequacy of some of the possible ones offered to us. The pathfinder is no more than a pathfinder; he is on his way through the jungle, but has not yet emerged into the clear light of day at the other side; he has been able to write 'cul-de-sac' at the entrance to some other attractive paths, but he has not yet been able to construct his own highroad; but he believes that he can see the goal distantly in front and takes courage to press on towards it.

What, then, have we discovered? First, we have seen that the roots of Christology lie in the application of categories from the Old Testament and Judaism to Jesus. In the period in question the influence of pagan ideas is minimal. Moreover, we have been able to account for the development very largely in terms of developments of thought that were possible in Palestine and Syria where the church began.

Second, we have found that behind the development there stands the figure of Jesus and the claims, indirect and direct, which he made for himself. The roots of Christology lie in the pre-Easter period in a stronger sense than Bultmann meant when he said that 'Jesus' call to decision implies a christology'.

Third, the evidence supports the view that it was the resurrection of Jesus which gave the decisive stimulus to Christological thinking. The firm recognition that Jesus was Lord and Messiah stemmed from the resurrection. The expectation of his parousia received credibility from his resurrection, and the Christological interpretation of his ministry likewise had its confirmation here. The earliest Christology stressed the way in which he fulfilled the Old Testament promises of a coming deliverer. It saw in Jesus the agent of God entrusted with the power to save and to judge, and it confessed him as the Lord to whom was given absolute authority. For these statements it was a short step to the application to him of the same authority and nature as God, and to the realization that, in whatever weak sense these traits might be seen in other messengers of God, he possessed them in a unique way as the Son of God. Functional Christology may well have preceded ontological

Christology, but the tendency in modern writers to separate them from each other is probably unjustified.

Fourth, the early church was not specifically concerned in the beginning with the divinity of Jesus; this emerged as the inescapable corollary of Jesus' position. But we can find no suggestion that it was the manhood of Jesus which was of greatest significance; it was the fact that he was the agent of God that mattered, that 'God was in Christ reconciling the world to himself'. The significance of his humanity was that God was really incarnate in human form; it was the Word that became flesh and so revealed the grace and truth of God. This fact has important consequences for modern understandings of Jesus in which his manhood is regarded as his most significant feature; despite the attempt to tell us that this was really what the early church was trying to say, it must be seriously questioned whether this approach does justice to the New Testament.[6] But here again is an issue that cannot be settled without more detailed examination.

## NOTES

[1] See O. Cullmann, *The Earliest Christian Confessions* (1949); V. H. Neufeld, *The Earliest Christian Confessions* (1963); R. Deichgräber, *Gotteshymnus und Christushymnus in der frühen Christenheit* (1967); J. T. Sanders, *The New Testament Christological Hymns* (1971).

[2] S. Schulz, *Q – die Spruchquelle der Evangelisten* (1972); G. N. Stanton, 'On the Christology of Q', in B. Lindars and S. S. Smalley, *Christ and Spirit in the New Testament* (1973), pp. 27-42.

[3] C. H. Dodd, *Historical Tradition in the Fourth Gospel* (1963). The scope of our study has precluded discussion of the title 'Word' (*Logos*) which figures so prominently in the prologue of John.

[4] For other treatments see L. Morris, *The Lord from Heaven* (1958); E. G. Jay, *Son of Man, Son of God* (1965); W. Marxsen, *The Beginnings of Christology* (1969); J. Ernst, *Anfänge der Christologie* (1972). Somewhat broader in scope is E. Schweizer, *Jesus* (1971). See also the appropriate sections in H. Conzelmann, *An Outline of the Theology of the New Testament* (1969), pp. 72-86, 127-137; W. G. Kümmel, *The Theology of the New Testament* (1974), pp. 58-85; 105-125.

[5] In other words, chapter 1 *was* written before the rest of the book.

[6] See J. A. T. Robinson, *The Human Face of God* (1972); D. Welbourn, *God-Dimensional Man* (1972).

# POSTSCRIPT

At the beginning of the final chapter of this book, headed
'An unfinished task', it was emphasized that there is a
danger in accepting the conclusions of a 'survey' type of
book as the last word on the subject. The stream of literature which has continued to appear during the years
since the original publication in 1976 confirms the truth
contained in this warning. What we must now ask is how far
the subsequent discussion has confirmed or questioned the
provisional conclusions offered then, and how far new questions have been raised and answered.

One of the points made early in the book was that it is
important to ask whether what we know of the historical
Jesus can bear the weight of the Christology which the early
church laid upon the foundation of its knowledge of him
and of his teaching.[1] This meant that we could not avoid the
question of the historical value of the Gospel material and
of the picture of Jesus contained within it. In particular, it
has often been argued that many of the sayings ascribed to
Jesus in the Gospels should really be attributed to early
Christian prophets who spoke in his name and on his
authority. M. E. Boring has produced a detailed study of
the nature of Christian prophecy and has analysed all the
sayings which in his view may not stem from Jesus himself
in their present form, in order to ascertain whether they
show the signs of Christian prophecy; he concludes that a
large number of sayings were modified or created in this
way.[2] This view had already been the subject of careful criti-

cism by D. Hill who argued for a much more limited scope
for finding prophetic material in the Gospels.[3] Then there
appeared the detailed work on early Christian prophecy by
D. E. Aune. Aune did not have access to the definitive edition of Boring's work, but on the basis of his earlier studies
he concluded that the historical evidence for the theory of
the prophetic origins of sayings in the Gospels 'lies largely
in the creative imagination of scholars'.[4] Over against such
theories much more weight should be given to the view that
Jesus himself acted as a teacher and that his disciples mem-
orized his sayings as they would have done those of any
other teacher.[5]

Our earlier discussion overlooked M. Hengel's important
study of *The Charismatic Leader and his Followers* in which he
protested against the historical scepticism with which some
scholars approach the Gospels as regards Jesus' self-
understanding. Starting from Matthew 8:21f. he showed
how Jesus cannot be understood purely on a rabbinic
model, but rather as a charismatic, prophetic and eschatological figure with a unique authority as the proclaimer of
the kingdom of God, one whose authority can be described
only as 'Messianic'. He comments: 'It seems very questionable to me whether we can go on adhering as a matter of
principle to the thesis, so popular at present, of a Jesus
wholly devoid of titles, given the unique "authority" of Jesus
which has its acme in the fact that he "dares to act in God's
stead".'[6]

A. E. Harvey has written a notable study of the historical
Jesus in which he claims that, by studying the historical constraints within which Jesus worked, we can appreciate more
fully the options open to him and assess more fully the
statements in the Gospels about him. Working in this manner, Harvey finds strong elements of history in the presentation of the death of Jesus and the trials surrounding it, his
prophetic stance against the law and his performance of
miracles. Harvey is not sure that the option of claiming to
be Messiah existed for Jesus, but he does see him as the
anointed messenger of Isaiah 61 and argues that 'Jesus
claimed (even if only implicitly) to be Son of God.'[7]

In these two books an attempt is made to work out the self-understanding of Jesus without reference to titles, but the clear implication of Hengel's work is that such a position is ultimately inconsistent and demands that we go further. Of the phrases in the Gospels that could represent titles used by Jesus, 'Son of man' is still the one which arouses the greatest hopes and the most vigorous controversy. A solid *Festschrift* in honour of A. Vögtle contained a number of contributions to the use of the phrase in the Gospels.[8] On the one hand, H. Schürmann and G. Schneider argue that the occurrences of the phrase in Q and the Lucan *Sondergut* are due not to Jesus but to the early church. On the other hand, W. G. Kümmel and R. Pesch argue for the use of the phrase by Jesus in Luke 12:8f.; Mark 9:31 and 14:62. A. J. B. Higgins, who contributed to the same volume, has also written a further monograph defending the Tödt-Hahn interpretation.[9] But the centre of interest in the English-speaking world is undoubtedly the further development of the kind of theory advanced by G. Vermes and discussed earlier in this book.[10] Two main contributions must be noted.

First, there is the detailed study of Daniel 7 and its influence by M. Casey.[11] Casey is primarily concerned with the original significance of Daniel 7; he argues that there is no 'Son of man' figure in the chapter, and that what we have is merely the use of a human figure as a symbol for Israel. In subsequent Jewish literature he finds (like Vermes and N. Perrin) that there is no Son of man concept. Then he looks at the Gospels. He argues that sayings which reflect the influence of Daniel 7 are not authentic teaching of Jesus. What survives is a set of some twelve texts, all of which can be translated back into Aramaic and which contain general statements using the Aramaic idiom *bar 'enash(a)* to make statements that were true of Jesus himself. Casey's discussion has the important merit of actually testing the possibility of Aramaic renditions of the texts.

Second, there is the study of B. Lindars who differs from his predecessors in arguing that the Aramaic idiom *bar 'enash(a)* refers not to people in general (and hence to the speaker in particular) but rather to a specific class of people with whom the speaker identifies himself.[12] He then claims that there is a core of authentic sayings in the Gospels which can be understood in this way. For example, in Matthew 8:20 Jesus says that foxes have holes and birds have nests, but he and anybody who shares in the conditions of his missionary vocation have no place of rest. This is one of the few sayings where the hypothesis looks credible and makes good sense of a saying; but when, for example, we are told that Jesus said, 'Just as Jonah was a sign to the Ninevites, . . . so there is a man who will be a sign to the present generation', or, again, that, if anybody confesses or denies Jesus now, he will have an advocate or an accuser in the shape of his own response to Jesus at the last judgment, our credulity is stretched to breaking point.

The work of these scholars suggests that instead of the usual threefold classification of the Son of man sayings[13] we should rather divide them into two basic groups – those which reflect an Aramaic idiom and those which show influence from Daniel 7. Is there any way of explaining the co-existence of these two types of saying? J. D. G. Dunn holds that it was Jesus himself who made the jump from the use of the Aramaic idiom to the use of an allusion to Daniel 7, and that once this jump was made the way was open for further use of Daniel 7.[14]

There have been other contributions to the study of the Son of man which require to be evaluated. S. Kim has advanced the interesting thesis that Jesus used 'Son of man' in line with its Danielic use (which was based in turn on Ezekiel 1) to refer to himself as a divine figure, the Son of God who is the head of the sons of God.[15] This hypothesis appeared independently of the works by Casey and Lindars and does not really come to terms with their discussion of the Aramaic background.

It will be evident that the Son of man problem is still giving rise to a great variety of answers. The concept of Messiahship by contrast has produced little discussion during the last ten years. It may well be that the concept of Son of man is essentially Messianic, as has been argued by different authors with reference to Daniel 7 and also to the use in the Gospels.[16]

We pass over the term 'Lord'[17] and come to the other title which has been the main focus of attention, Son of God. In 1977 there appeared a symposium entitled *The Myth of God Incarnate* in which a number of British authors argued that the concept of incarnation is not central to the New Testament teaching about Jesus, that it represents a use of mythological language derived from the religious environment of early Christianity, and that it is an unnecessary and misleading mythological expression for contemporary theology; it needs to be replaced by other conceptions of Jesus.[18] The book aroused considerable controversy.[19] What made it all the more controversial was that it was compiled by a number of scholars who held ministerial office in various churches (five of the seven were Anglicans) but who were hardly upholding the creeds of Christendom in anything like their plain sense. In reality a lot hangs on how 'myth' is defined. Few would deny that language about divine sonship is analogical, and, if nothing more than this is meant by the use of the misleading and highly ambiguous term 'myth', then perhaps no great harm is being done. But the contributors obviously meant more than this, and were concerned to deny that this was helpful or meaningful language. Christians who feel that the guidance – dare we say, the authority – of Scripture must be taken seriously may think otherwise, and in any case it is far from obvious that the language of incarnation is meaningless except to followers of Bultmann's outmoded view of a closed universe in which a real incarnation is impossible. So the question comes down to whether incarnation is taught in the New Testament.

The most important discussion of this theme is undoubtedly that of J. D. G. Dunn.[20] It takes the form of a detailed discussion of all the major Christological titles and categories which might be thought to contain the notion of pre-existence and hence of incarnation. Dunn argues that what we normally understand by pre-existence is not found in any of the New Testament writings prior to the Johan-

nine corpus. He claims that the texts in which it is commonly found have been misinterpreted. In reality they refer
to the human self-sacrifice of Jesus (Phil. 2:5–11) or to the
way in which God's creative power, once manifested in Wisdom, is now manifested in Jesus. Only in John is there gen-
uinely the concept of a pre-existent being who has come
into the world and assumed flesh. For Dunn this is sufficient
to show that the concept of incarnation is not derived from
myth and is not in itself mythological, and he clearly retains
the concept as an integral part of his Christology. But, despite his attempts to justify his position,[21] it is very dubious
whether he has succeeded in purging the non-Johannine
literature of the concepts of pre-existence and incarnation.[22]

One cannot conclude this review without going back to a
book published at the beginning of the period in 1977 by
C. F. D. Moule, who boldly wrote: 'I am concerned to challenge, in the name of the evidence, such a statement as that
"the fundamental problem of a Christology of the NT ...
was that the view of Jesus found in NT Christology was *not
historically true of Jesus himself*"' (my italics).[23] Moule argues
that in much recent writing we can find an evolutionary
view of New Testament doctrine in which new species
appear in course of time, and he defends by contrast a
developmental view, according to which later growth simply
brings out more clearly what was latent and implicit from
the beginning. This is not to deny that the New Testament
authors were real theologians with creative powers, as is
sometimes suggested by radical critics of conservative
standpoints; it is rather to insist that the New Testament
theologians worked in the consciousness that they were
defenders and expounders of a tradition which had
authority over them. Moule discusses the use of Christological terms in the Gospels and argues that in each case
the use of the terms was dictated by what Jesus himself was.
He then examines what Christ meant in the experience of
the early church, and here he devotes attention to the
understanding of Jesus in corporate terms, an experience
which could be explained only by the use of terms appropri-

ate to God himself. This is a fresh and stimulating approach to the topic.

Here we must break off our account of the ongoing story. We have confined our attention in this Postcript to the topics discussed earlier in the book. It goes without saying that they cover only a part of Christology.[24] They are, however, concerned with the foundations, and it is only if this part of the work is done well that we shall be able to proceed further with confidence. It has emerged that the questions of the Aramaic background to 'Son of man' and of the basis for the church's doctrine of the incarnation of the pre-existent Word have come to the forefront in recent study. If scholars remain as far from a consensus on these and other topics as they were in 1976, it can nevertheless be maintained that there are still good scholarly reasons for affirming the general view of the development of New Testament Christology which we then put forward as a provisional solution.

## NOTES

[1]   See above, p. 13.
[2]   M. E. Boring, *Sayings of the Risen Jesus* (Society for New Testament Studies Monograph Series 46; Cambridge University Press, 1982); 'Christian Prophecy and the Sayings of Jesus: the State of the Question', *NTS* 29, 1983, pp. 104-112.
[3]   D. Hill, *New Testament Prophecy* (London: Marshall, Morgan & Scott, 1979).
[4]   D. E. Aune, *Prophecy in Early Christianity and the Ancient Mediterranean World* (Grand Rapids: Eerdmans, 1983), p. 245.
[5]   R. Riesner, *Jesus als Lehrer* (Wissenschaftliche Untersuchungen zum Neuen Testament 2:7; Tübingen: J. C. B. Mohr, 1981).
[6]   M. Hengel, *The Charismatic Leader and his Followers* (Edinburgh: T. & T. Clark, 1981), p. 71. Needless to say, Hengel's stress that Jesus is not to be understood *primarily* on a rabbinic analogy does not invalidate Riesner's thesis.
[7]   A. E. Harvey, *Jesus and the Constraints of History* (London: Duckworth, 1982), p. 171.
[8]   R. Pesch and R. Schnackenburg (eds.), *Jesus und der Menschensohn* (Freiburg: Herder, 1975).
[9]   A. J. B. Higgins, *The Son of Man in the Teaching of Jesus* (Society for New Testament Studies Monograph Series 39; Cambridge University Press, 1980).
[10]   See above, pp. 64f.
[11]   M. Casey, *Son of Man* (London: SPCK, 1979).
[12]   B. Lindars, *Jesus Son of Man* (London: SPCK, 1983).
[13]   See above, p. 69.
[14]   J. D. G. Dunn, *Christology in the Making* (London: SCM Press, 1980, [2]1989), pp. 86-88.
[15]   S. Kim, 'The "Son of Man" ' as the Son of God (Tübingen: J. C. B. Mohr, 1983).
[16]   G. R. Beasley-Murray, 'The Interpretation of Daniel 7', *CBQ* 45, 1983, pp.

44-58; G. Gerleman, *Der Menschensohn* (Studia Biblica 1; Leiden: E. J. Brill, 1983). See further G. R. Beasley-Murray, *Jesus and the Kingdom of God* (Grand Rapids: Eerdmans, 1986); C. C. Caragounis, *The Son of Man* (Tübingen: J. C. B. Mohr, 1986).

[17] J. A. Fitzmyer, 'Der semitische Hintergrund des neutestamentlichen Kyriostitels', in G. Strecker (ed.), *Jesus Christus in Historie und Theologie* (Tübingen: J. C. B. Mohr, 1975), pp. 267-298.

[18] J. Hick (ed.), *The Myth of God Incarnate* (London: SCM Press, 1977).

[19] M. Green (ed.), *The Truth of God Incarnate* (London: Hodder & Stoughton, 1977); G. Carey, *God Incarnate* (Leicester: Inter-Varsity Press, 1977); M. Goulder (ed.), *Incarnation and Myth: The Debate Continued* (London: SCM Press, 1979). See further my essay 'God Incarnate: Myth or What?' which together with various other previously published essays appears in I. H. Marshall, *Jesus the Saviour: Studies in New Testament Theology* (London: SPCK / Downers Grove: InterVarsity Press, 1990).

[20] See above, n. 14.

[21] *Ibid.*, pp. xi-xxxi; *cf.* 'In Defence of a Methodology', *Exp.T* 95, 1983–84, pp. 295-299.

[22] I. H. Marshall, 'Incarnational Christology in the New Testament', in H. H. Rowdon (ed.), *Christ the Lord* (Leicester: Inter-Varsity Press, 1982), pp. 1-16; see also S. Kim, *The Origin of Paul's Gospel* (Tübingen: J. C. B. Mohr, 1981), for a different approach to the material from that of Dunn.

[23] C. F. D. Moule, *The Origin of Christology* (Cambridge University Press, 1977).

[24] In an important essay ('Toward the Renewal of New Testament Christology', *NTS* 32, 1986, pp. 362-377), L. E. Keck has pointed out the dangers of concentrating attention simply on Christological titles and rightly indicated the need for a broader approach. For a fresh survey of the field see M. de Jonge, *Christology in Context: The Earliest Christian Response to Jesus* (Philadelphia: Westminster Press, 1988).

# INDEX